OTHER BOOKS BY DOUGLAS FAIRBAIRN

A Man's World
The Voice of Charlie Pont
A Gazelle on the Lawn
A Squirrel of One's Own
Shoot

A Squirrel Forever

by Douglas Fairbairn

ILLUSTRATED BY BETTY FRASER

Simon and Schuster · New York

Copyright © 1973 by Douglas Fairbairn
All rights reserved
including the right of reproduction
in whole or in part in any form
Published by Simon and Schuster
Rockefeller Center, 630 Fifth Avenue
New York, New York 10020

SBN 671-21587-6
Library of Congress Catalog Card Number: 73-7924
Designed by Irving Perkins
Manufactured in the United States of America
Printed by Mahoney & Roese, Inc., New York, N.Y.
Bound by American Book-Stratford Press, Inc., New York, N.Y.

1 2 3 4 5 6 7 8 9 10

Part One

509-121848

One In july 1965 I saved an infant female gray squirrel from a neighbor's cat. The cat had found the helpless bit of gray fluff out in the woods and was planning to toy with her for a while and then eat her up. I happened to look out the window of my house in Florida at a most fortunate moment, saw what was on the agenda, sneaked up on the cat and snatched its prize away.

Miraculously, the squirrel was completely unharmed. Besides, she had full fur, otherwise she probably would not have survived. My intentions were good, but I knew very little about animals of any kind, much less wild ones, and I needed all the luck I could get in my first few frantic days of playing mother squirrel to the baby. I fed her warm milk with a little sugar in it from an eyedropper every four hours or so (as I had been instructed to do by a girl on the switchboard at the Humane Society, which I had called almost in hysteria the evening of the rescue), and she survived. In less than a week she was playing with me and beginning to explore my house.

I think she was about a month and a half old when I saved her from the cat. That is roughly the age, I found out at the library, when gray squirrels get full fur. They are born naked and about the size of the middle joint of your little finger, in litters of two or three, usually twice a year. Normally they are weaned at about two months, and I firmly resolved to return my squirrel to the woods the minute she went off milk. For one thing, I simply didn't want to have a pet of any kind—didn't want the responsibility, didn't want to be tied down, didn't want the mess, didn't want the hassle—and besides, I was very much opposed, as a matter of principle, to the idea of keeping a wild animal in captivity.

In the meantime, I named her Chippy.

At first I kept her in a nest of towels in the bottom of a beach bag. But as she grew stronger and more active day by day, her capacity for getting into dangerous situations around the house increased dramatically, and soon I had to confine her most of the time, for her own good, in an improvised cage made of an upside-down plastic laundry basket. That didn't last long. Chippy gnawed her way to freedom in a couple of days, and then it was the bathroom. That didn't last long either. A squirrel in your bathroom is not an unmixed blessing. For instance, to have one run joyously up your leg as you step from the shower is a shattering experience. And that sort of thing wasn't the worst of it. In there, with all those hard edges of tile and chromium fixtures to hurt herself on and all those bottles and tubes to knock over and bite into, Chippy was an endless worry to me.

Soon I had to make a difficult decision: whether to let her go while she was still living mostly on milk and hope that she would be able to make it on her own in the wild, or build her a real cage. In the end, I went to a lumber company and bought a six-foot by seven-foot section of wire fence with openings one inch by two inches and tied the ends together to form a cylinder. When I stood the thing up on its end and put a piece of screen over the top I had a circular cage six feet tall and seven feet in circumference.

The irony of it all was that it was on the very day that I made the cage and put Chippy in it that she refused milk for the first time. When I tried to give her her seven-o'clock bottle through the bars she just wouldn't take it. From then on it was strictly grown-up squirrel food, and I was left with my firm resolution hanging in the air. I knew that I should have turned her loose right then. I was positive that she could have survived. But I had grown fond of her.

Too fond. Too attached. Too charmed. Too fascinated by everything about her.

I made a new resolution—that I would keep her just a little while longer. Not for long, certainly not forever. Just a little while.

Then time went by and Chippy and I became good friends. She didn't mind her cage once she got used to it. I kept it filled with fresh oak branches for her to gnaw on and do acrobatics on, and I built her a little house and hung it from a branch near the top of the cage. Every evening she disappeared into the house, curled up in a ball with her tail over her and usually slept straight through until dawn, when she came out and began another day's activities. She spent most of each morning exercising by running around and around in her cage, nibbling on leaves, lettuce, ferns, flowers, corn, peanuts and sunflower seeds, washing her tail and her fur with moisture from her nose and grooming her tail by combing it out with her two long lower teeth. Over and over she hid sunflower seeds in the newspaper at the bottom of her cage until, by her mysterious calculations, she found exactly the right spot for each one.

I let her out of the cage for a few hours every day, in the late morning and again in the afternoon, and we played a set of squirrel-in-the-tree, a game in which she was the squirrel and I was the tree, and she ran all over me at high speed, alternately chasing my hands and being chased by them. When she tired of that she went on to the more serious business of grooming her tail some more, prowling silently through the rooms to make sure that no owls or hawks or falcons had sneaked into the house while her back had been turned and carefully hiding dozens of sunflower seeds in every crack and corner.

It was a peaceable kingdom. I lived on a densely wooded coral ridge overlooking a bay, a sort of tropical rain forest in which there lived beautiful birds, squirrels, a pair of handsome gray foxes, several opossums, some raccoons and a fair number of semi-feral cats. Since all of the people I knew were aware that I was working on a long novel and needed plenty of solitude, they left me pretty much alone, and Chippy and I led a quiet life. Inevitably I grew fonder, more attached, more charmed, more fascinated every day, and I kept pushing the whole question of when I would let her go farther and farther back in my mind until most of the time I stopped thinking about it altogether.

And then, suddenly, our relationship took a very bad turn. It was all because of the hard-shelled nuts. In October the stores were full of pecans, walnuts, brazils and filberts, and I brought them home to my squirrel by the bagful, happily, innocently, and she took them all and treasured them and ate a few and hid the rest until the whole house started turning lumpy with her pecans, walnuts, brazils and filberts. It went on this way for many months because I thought it was fun and thought Chippy thought it was fun and also because it was the only way I knew of to spoil her—and I wanted to spoil her a little. But gradually her excitement over the nuts gave way to hysteria, paranoia and megalomania, and she began to see me not as the *giver* of nuts but as the *taker away* of nuts. Then one day in May she attacked me savagely when she thought I had come too close to one of her caches.

After that she attacked me several more times, fiercely, bloodily and usually without any warning. I decided that she would have to go, because it seemed to me that the real meaning of the attacks was that she was trying to tell me in her own way that she wanted to go.

Still, deciding to let Chippy go and actually letting her go were two different things, and I kept putting it off on one pretext or another all through the rest of the summer and into the fall. At last one fine morning in September, when she had lived in my house for a little over a year and had turned so mean that I couldn't even let her out of her cage any more, I knew that the time had come. Impulsively I picked up her cage and carried it outside and across a field to a line of big oaks, where I set it down under a low branch and let Chippy out. She ran ecstatically up into the trees, an immensely happy squirrel reveling in her first freedom. I stayed and watched her for a long time, until I lost her among the other squirrels. Then I returned to my empty house, thinking that probably I would never see her again. I knew that I would miss her, and I did miss her terribly, but I was glad that she was free and sure that she would make it on her own.

However, that night there was a storm, with thunder and

lightning and buckets of rain, and the next evening, purely by chance, I saw a bedraggled squirrel gazing at me from a branch of a tree about halfway between the oaks and my house. It was Chippy, and it was clear that she had had about all the freedom she wanted. There was nothing I could do but take her home.

Two   WHAT A curious sight I must have been, bringing Chippy home—carrying her in the big cage, walking sideways because that was how I had to do it in order to be able to see where I was going, bent slightly backward by the cage's top-heavy weight. My fingers were killing me where they were laced through the stiff wire openings of the cage, and I was huffing and puffing, red in the face– maybe even purple—while inside the cage the squirrel bounced along like a little maharajah riding in one of those things that the maharajahs ride in on the backs of elephants.

For some reason I had felt that the right way for her to return was not on my shoulder, which would have been a lot easier, but as she had left—in her cage. I figured that this might make her understand what coming home really meant, that if I brought the cage to her and she saw it and remembered it and hated it now after her taste of freedom, never wanting any part of it again, she would just turn away and disappear back into the trees and that would be the end of it. Anyway, instead of inviting her to hop onto my shoulder, I had gone back across the field, retrieved the cage from under the oak trees where I had left it the day before when I had set her free and put it down close to the branch where she was lying watching me. Then I opened the door—which was actually just a twelve-inch by six-inch section of the cage itself that I had cut out with wire cutters, hinged on the left with four clothespins and fastened on the right with one—and waited to see what would happen. She gazed at the cage for a moment and then jumped onto my shoulder, ran down the back of my shirt and my pants leg, made a small but expressive puddle on the ground, ran back up to my shoulder and hopped from there through the door and into her cage. That had been good enough for me, and I had closed the door and picked up the cage and started off toward my house, slowly and painfully.

I went along the driveway and across the lawn, up a short flight of stone steps, under a trellis covered with red bougainvillaea and hung along both sides (in baskets) with six or seven kinds of ferns and wild tree lilies from the Everglades, across a balustraded terrace of coral rock and grass and up another flight of steps to the balcony outside my front door. Carrying the cage up the steps was not only awkward but dangerous, because there was always the possibility of losing my balance, toppling over and crashing to the ground, cage, squirrel and all. And then perhaps when I finally did reach the balcony I might not be able to swing the door open because the cage was in the way and I would have to stagger back down to the terrace, leave the cage, go back up and open the door and then go back down and get the cage again.

In the end, though, the cage stood once more in the corner of the living room where it had always stood. I opened the door and stuck my hand in, and Chippy, instead of running at it ferociously as she most certainly would have done a couple of days before, rubbed her face along my hand to encourage me to scratch her nose. Finally she stuck her whole head into the hollow of my hand and lay stretched out on one of the oak branches inside the cage with her body absolutely limp and her long and lovely (if somewhat matted at the moment) tail drooping.

Looking at her, I remembered how vicious she had been in the weeks before I had let her go, and I couldn't help wondering how long this would last. Would she be her old impossible self in the morning, clicking her teeth at me, growling at me in a squirrel's growl, which is a sort of faint, insistent and thoroughly unnerving moan, flinging herself against the side of her cage any time I came near it and in general acting as if she would like to tear me apart?

Too often in the past I had seen her go from affection to ferocity in the blink of an eye to trust her present mood very far.

And yet I was glad to have her home. It made me happy to look at her and touch her again and to see her cage back in its familiar place. Her presence gave me the feeling that things had returned to normal, that all was well, that the good old days were back again. There was no denying that there was something genuinely endearing about the idea that she had gone out into the world and seen it all and had wanted to come back to me.

And so I was rather in the position of the person who sincerely wants to give up a habit, thinks about it for a long time, broods over it, agonizes, makes a thousand false starts and then one day finally does give it up. He goes through the tortures of hell but feels good anyway because he knows that it had to be done sooner or later. But then he suddenly weakens and goes back to the habit, whatever it was, and wallows in remorse, guilt, despair and joy.

Chippy lay with her face in my hand for about five minutes, and then, abruptly, as if something important had just occurred to her, she sat up straight and stared at me. A moment later she ran head first down the inside of her cage to the floor. She dashed around the perimeter of the cage and then ran back up and looked at me reproachfully.

Our sentimental interlude was over. She was starving, and there wasn't even a bit of lettuce on the floor. So I went to the refrigerator and shucked an ear of corn.

Lately she had begun to like fresh corn more than anything else, and when I brought the corn to her and was still halfway across the room she would go wild at the smell. She would take the cob from me eagerly and, sitting up and holding it in front of her, begin eating in her quick, intense, nervous way. And yet, as hungry as she was, she was still precise. She would eat one row all the way around, making an incision along the center of each kernel, then pull the kernel loose from the cob and in one motion scoop out the pulp with her teeth and eject the thin shell of the kernel from the side of her mouth with her tongue. When she came to the end of the first row she would start on the next one.

While she was dealing with the corn I checked her house to see if it was dry. Luckily, when the rain had started the night before I had gone out and thrown a slicker over the top of the cage. This had kept the rain out of her house and had also kept the beach towels dry that were spread over the screen on top of the cage. I removed the slicker and, with Chippy still munching away inside, lifted the cage out of the corner. I put some newspapers on the floor in the corner, placed a few leaves of lettuce, a piece of orange and a handful of sunflower seeds on the newspapers and lifted the cage back.

At this point Chippy dropped her corn to the floor with a thud, slipped out of the open doorway of her cage, climbed up on top and gave herself a thorough drying off by lying first on one side and then on the other and plowing around in circles on the beach towels. Then she burrowed deep into the towels and made a tremendous upheaval as she pretended that she was trapped and couldn't find her way out. Finally, she reappeared, sat up on a clump of towels with a very solemn look on her face and started grooming her tail. She grabbed hold of the bush roughly with both hands, pulled it to her nose and, snorting and sneezing, washed it with her nose from end to end and combed it out with her teeth. She did a thorough job, and when she was finished her tail was light and fluffy and beautiful again.

After that she climbed back into the cage and, without another look at me, retired to her house.

Usually when she went to bed she fussed for a while with the pieces of towel I had given her for bedding before she settled down, because she was a squirrel who liked a comfortable bed, particularly a soft pillow. I would hear her thumping in there against the ceiling and the walls of her house as she turned around and around, arranging and rearranging, making sure that everything was satisfactory. But this time she just dived into the box, made one circle and called it a night.

At about that time the wind came up, and it started raining again. For a long time I sat in the living room in the growing darkness, listening to the rain and thinking about my squirrel and me. I had common sense enough to know that I should have passed her by when I had seen her lying on the branch waiting for me. To be cold-blooded about it, the disadvantages of being a squirrel owner far outweighed the advantages. The advantages were all a thing of the spirit, but the disadvantages were real, day to day and endless. Taking care of Chippy on the basic level of cleaning her cage and keeping her supplied with food and water wasn't actually very arduous or tedious or unpleasant, but it took time and had to be done regularly and scrupulously. On the more personal level, playing with her and overseeing her when she was out of her cage and mousing around on her own in the house, wasn't too much trouble either, but it also took time and patience. And none of it was anything I could delegate to someone else, even if I wanted to get out of it now and then. She simply wasn't like the ordinary sort of pet—dogs or cats, turtles or goldfish or canaries—that almost everyone has had some experience with at one time or another and could just hand over to someone and know that it would be taken care of at least adequately. Everything about Chippy was unusual, and to get along with her and treat her right you had to care about her and understand her, and there was nobody like that except me. All of which tied me down to the extent that I couldn't even go away on an overnight trip and hadn't during the whole year that she had been with me.

On top of that, there was the problem of what to do with Chippy if she got sick. I had already discovered that it was difficult to find a veterinarian who knew anything about treating wild animals. When Chippy had fallen on her head when she was still very young and had suffered a mild concussion, I had had to call the lion doctor at a zoo to ask for advice. And even if there was a local veterinarian who was experienced with wild animals, the question was how I could ever get Chippy to him and, if I did, how the man could ever hope to examine her and treat her when that would certainly mean handling her and I could barely do that myself.

But common sense and cold blood mean nothing, of course, when it comes to affection and strong attachments, and so I had not been able to pass Chippy by. Now there she was back in her cage in the corner of the living room, full of corn and sleeping peacefully, and there I was right back where I had started. I couldn't help remembering the first night that Chippy had spent in my house, and I hadn't been able to get over the idea that down inside the beach bag beside my bed a baby squirrel was sleeping.

Before I went to bed the night of Chippy's return, I did something that I hadn't dared do in a long time. I visited her in her house. Visiting meant opening the door of the cage, reaching up and putting my hand into her house. Before she had turned mean I had done it all the time. Afterward I had been afraid to. It was only when she was in her house that she felt totally secure and relaxed all of her fantastically sensitive alert mechanisms. In fact, it was only when she was in her house that she would even close her eyes. The rest of the time they were always popped wide open and almost never blinked. It was strange to feel her off her guard and completely limp, untremulous and at ease, all warm velvet fur.

When I put my hand into the box she didn't stir. She was sleeping in one of her favorite positions, on her back, her nose in the air, her head on a lump of towel, her hands folded across her chest, her tail covering her eyes and her back feet resting on the ceiling.

Well, she did move a little—just enough to give me a quick warning nip on the tip of one of my fingers. But that was what she had always done when I had first entered her house even in the best of times, and I was thankful anyway that it wasn't the wild attack that I had been dreading and half anticipating.

Squirrels have no sense of proportion. When my hand was in her house, as far as Chippy was concerned I was in her house, and I don't think she could ever understand why, once I was in there, I just didn't settle down and stay the night. On cold or stormy nights she would put on a great display of squirrel hospitality by fluffing up her tail and laying it over my hand. It made a super blanket, as light as air but marvelously warm, and it was easy for me to see how squirrels can survive in even the bitterest cold weather, curled up in the hollow of a tree with their tails pulled over them.

I stroked her nose and tickled behind her ears and tugged gently at her lower lip, which was something she liked very much, and she snoozed happily away. But when I finally got tired of holding my arm up and started to pull my hand out of her house, she instantly grabbed hold of my thumb with both hands and took the tip firmly between her teeth, which was her way of telling me not to be silly, to be still, to be happy there with her, to go to sleep. It was raining, wasn't it? The wind was howling, wasn't it? Obviously the only place to be on a night like this was safe in a squirrel's house.

Chippy slept for almost two days straight. She came out of her house occasionally for a nibble of corn or fruit or a few sunflower seeds and then went right back to bed.

On the third day everything returned to normal. When I got up in the morning she was on her rounds—running up and down her cage at full speed. Around ten o'clock I let her out, and we had a good brisk game of squirrel-in-the-tree.

Then she went off to explore the house, while I cleaned her cage. In the afternoon I did some work on my book in the living room and Chippy played by herself all over the room. In the late afternoon, as was her way, she turned thoughtful and lay on a branch in her cage, gazing out the window for a long time, until dusk, when she got up and went silently into her house. Soon I heard the faint thumping of her head against the walls and the ceiling as she fussed with her bedding.

And so we took up our old life again, and we were happy, but from time to time I would stop and think about the situation, and all of my old apprehensions would come back. What had happened before, I thought, would happen again. I felt sure of it. Actually, I was waiting for it, watching for the first signs of it, unconsciously. One of these days Chippy would turn on me again. And then what?

Three   ONE DAY, about three weeks after she had gone away and come back, Chippy, ever the good watch squirrel, made a startling discovery.

We were both in the living room at the time. It was in the afternoon. I was reading, she was running around the room on the picture molding—the narrow strip of molding you find in the rooms of old houses (which mine was), from which you were meant to hang pictures, thus saving knocking holes in the plaster with nails. She would go chugging around and around the room like a little locomotive for an hour or two at a time, occasionally jumping down from the molding onto the top of a cabinet or her cage to hide in a new place a seed or a nut she had found in an old place.

I wasn't paying much attention to her—you couldn't; it would give you vertigo to watch her—but all of a sudden from the corner of my eye I saw her hop from the molding to the top of her cage, run halfway down the side of the cage and jump from there over onto the windowsill on the south side of the room. There she froze, standing up straight and tall on her hind legs, with her head cocked attentively to one side and her hands curled inward to her chest, the image of concentration.

One of my problems with Chippy was that I could never resist her when she went into a full alert. I had to drop whatever I was doing and try to see for myself what it was that she saw. The trouble was that nine times out of ten there simply was nothing to see, or at least nothing that I could see. And yet, to look at her, you would have thought that a flying saucer had just landed in the driveway. And when I did see something it usually turned out to be a cardinal digging in the leaves down below or a cat sharpening its claws on the root of a tree. I got fooled time after time, but I kept coming back for more.

I watched her for a minute to see if she was really serious, and then I put my magazine aside, went to the window and stood beside Chippy, looking where she seemed to be looking. But that was another problem. It's almost impossible to tell where a squirrel is looking. Their eyes are like little shiny black marbles without whites around them, and it is only when you look at them closely in bright sunlight that you can see that actually the iris is a very dark liquid brown and just the pupil itself is black. At any rate, their eyes never seem to move or to be looking in any particular direction (or, to put it in a different way, they always seem to be looking in every direction at once). The fact is that squirrels have such superb peripheral vision that they can see simultaneously almost everything above, below, in front of and behind them without having to move either their eyes or their heads. (Their blind spots are directly behind their heads and directly in front of their noses. Squirrels can't see what they're eating, but their highly sensitive noses tell them all they need to know.)

Chippy was standing in profile to the window, which meant that only her left eye was looking outside. (I had noticed that when she really wanted to concentrate on something she looked at it sideways with one eye rather than head on with both.) Her head was cocked toward the sunken garden, but I couldn't see anything down there.

The sunken garden was a large natural depression in the coral rock of the ridge, and it was more a garden of colossal trees than of anything else because almost nothing could grow in the deep shade of the trees. The floor of the garden was about eight feet below the general level of the ground on the ridge. The walls on three sides were irregular terraces of sharp-edged rock. In the other wall, which was perpendicular, was a small cave. The walls and floor of the garden were covered with ferns and tangled philodendron vines. Steps made of rock and slapped-on cement went down into the garden, leading to a crude well house, also made of rock and cement, which had a pointed roof on top and inside an old electric Jacuzzi pump that still worked like a charm when you turned it on even though it hadn't been in regular service since the town had gone on the public water system around 1950. Stuck in the gobs of cement here and there all over the house were little porcelain blue jays, cardinals and robins, and growing out of a hole in the roof was a large plant with thick, waxy leaves that was nothing much to look at most of the year but for one glorious week or so in the spring burst forth with sprays of extraordinarily beautiful salmon-colored blooms.

Out of the garden five big oak trees grew, along with a golden shower (a flowering tree that once a year filled the air with thousands of golden petals whenever the wind blew), a gumbo limbo, an ironwood tree, a sapodilla and a cannonball tree—an import from Latin America of such extreme vulnerability that it instantly lost every one of its pale-green leaves at the slightest change in the temperature, either upward or downward. (Someone told me once that maracas are made from the gourds that grow very slowly on the trunks—on the trunks, not the branches—of the cannonball tree. They are big green balls, one or two a year, that turn dark and hard when they ripen.) The tenacious philodendrons climbed up the trees, reaching with them higher and higher, their vines as thick as ships' cables and their leaves immense and waving like battle flags up at the very tops of the trees where they caught the sun and the wind.

Chippy kept on staring down (presumably) into the garden, and I, staring with her and attuned to a certain degree to the ways of the wild from having lived with her so long, automatically listened for the blue jays. I knew that if there was something evil happening anywhere on the property—if a cat had caught a bird, or if the marsh hawk that lived in a pine down in front had caught a bird or a squirrel, or if a strange hawk or owl had suddenly been discovered in our midst—if it was something like that that was bothering Chippy, the blue jays would soon know about it. They would sound the alarm that would bring all the other birds flying so that they could all gang together and try to screech the miscreant straight out of its mind. But the jays were silent.

I was about to write Chippy off as an alarmist and go back to my magazine when I saw something move in the mouth of the little cave in the sunken garden. The windows in the living room looked across the garden to the cave, but the mouth was heavily obscured by vines. I couldn't imagine what I might have seen. It had been just a quick movement, a flash of red or brown. I looked at Chippy and I could tell that she had seen it too. She was staring so intently now that she was leaning far over, and her eyeball was almost touching the window.

Then I saw something else, and it made my heart skip a beat. The male gray fox was standing in the driveway.

The driveway was a narrow lane of asphalt—crumbling at the edges and full of bumps and cracks where the roots of the trees were writhing under it—that ran through the exact middle of the property, dividing to go around the ancient heart-shaped swimming pool, joining again, and then plunging down the front slope of the ridge toward the bay. It passed right by the sunken garden. In fact, the cave was directly below the driveway. With its arched entrance it looked somewhat like a natural culvert in the rock.

The fox was standing at a point on the driveway above the mouth of the cave. Had he been there all along? I knew that it was possible because the same thing had happened several times before, and it always gave me an eerie feeling to find that I had been looking at him and hadn't even known it. Anyway, it was the first time I had ever seen him stand still for so long out in the open, and I thought there must be a very good reason for him to be taking such a chance.

Then I had the feeling that if I looked around a bit, knowing what I was looking for now, having already spotted the male, I would see the female somewhere close by. It seemed that they were never far apart, because when you saw one you would likely see the other. So I looked along the driveway, and there she was. Had she been there all along too?

I had become rather fond of the foxes in the couple of months that I had been seeing them around the property. I had first begun seeing them at night, in the headlights of my car when I came home late. But then I had begun seeing them in the evening and the early morning. There was a special place where they liked to sun themselves in the morning. It was a small cleared place with tall grass in front that screened it from the driveway and dense brush behind that they could slip away into if they sensed danger. In the early morning the sun fell on the cleared place, and the male fox would sit up on his haunches with his nose lifted to smell the wind, while the little female would either lie beside him or busily wash his face and throat.

I caught sight of them one morning when I was walking along the driveway and just happened to look in their direction when I was at a point where it was possible to see through the tall grass to the cleared place. After that I had known where to look for them, and they had almost always been there at the same time, when the sun was slanting down at the same angle through the trees. At other times I would see them running in the field or along the driveway, but just a glimpse. When I saw them they would know instantly somehow that they had been seen, and they would vanish.

They looked terribly thin. I wondered if they were getting enough to eat. And they ran with a nervous gait that always made them appear dead tired and perhaps desperate.

To add to my worries about them, at night I would hear guns firing along the ridge and in the wide field down by the bay, and I knew that the slaughter of our wildlife was continuing.

The fact was that the ridge had suddenly (within the past couple of years) found itself squarely in the path of progress. Every day more people were moving into the area, and the ridge had felt the first shock of the great wave of building that was so rapidly transforming the whole lower east coast of Florida. The old houses that had basked in the pure sunlight for fifty years or more were being demolished one by one, and the oak forest that had covered the ridge was being cut down. To the north of my house dozens of new houses had been built, and to the south the battlements of high-rise apartments had begun to appear above the tops of the trees. The noise and dust of heavy construction filled the air, and the roads were jammed with traffic.

I am not against progress. All I'm saying is that I was worried about the foxes. Before, people had seemed to consider the wildlife on the ridge as much a part of the environment as the trees, the grass or the clouds in the sky and had simply not given much thought to the opossums, foxes and raccoons that had lived in our midst. The new people thought about them a good deal—as vermin, as carriers of rabies and as good targets. So they went out at night with lights and shot at them, and during the day their poodles, boxers, shepherds, Dobermans, terriers and Weimaraners ran in packs through the neighborhood, treeing the opossums and raccoons and running the foxes to distraction. And day and night the cars left small, furry bodies on the roads.

If I could have spoken to the foxes I would have told them to stay right there on the property, where I was king, and I would not have let any harm come to them either by rifle or by fang. I would have told them not to dare leave, not to cross the roads, not to go down to the field by the bay, where I most certainly was not king, or that would be the end of them and their magnificent bushy tails.

But of course I couldn't speak to them. I couldn't even get near enough to them to try to convey my central idea, which was that if they would just do things my way I would provide them with chicken necks beyond their wildest dreams. (I had found out from some of the old-timers on the ridge—who, if they really trusted you, would admit that they too liked the foxes and were worried about them and had a couple living on their property that they were trying to look out for—that the thing foxes liked more than anything else on earth was chicken necks, and I had laid in a big supply.) In my icebox I had one package of chicken necks still frozen, one thawing and one ready to go, but whenever I went out with a batch and placed them around where I thought the foxes would be sure to come across them, they had just stayed there until the flies and the cats had gotten them.

Now, as I stood with Chippy at the window, trying to figure out what was going on—why the foxes were standing in the open in the driveway—I saw another quick movement in the cave and then another and another. Things seemed to be flying back and forth behind the vines. Then, suddenly, a face poked through the vines and looked out at the sunken garden, and the mystery was solved. It was the gorgeous face of a baby fox. A moment later two other little faces came into view.

I was dumfounded—to think that, absolutely unknown to me, three fox kits had been born practically under my nose. It was hard to believe and harder still when I remembered that not once had I ever seen either the male or the female fox go into or come out of the garden.

The three kits started wrestling, rolling over and over in the mouth of the cave. The male fox listened anxiously to the thrashing about below him, his ears pricked and dancing in circles so that he could look in every direction for danger. In his nervousness he appeared almost to be standing on tiptoe. Then the mother passed behind him and went down into the garden. I saw her disappear into the cave, and she must have taken stern measures, because the youngsters quieted down immediately and there wasn't a sign of life behind the vines.

The little man hung around in the driveway for a few minutes and then, apparently satisfied that all was well for the moment anyway, trotted off into the underbrush on the other side of the driveway, to stand guard, I imagined, from cover.

I think that I just happened to have had the luck to be watching when the kits had no longer been able to contain their explosive youthful energy. Until then the parents had been able to keep them under control, but now their exuberance had finally bubbled over and they wanted to run and play and tussle and, certainly, to say goodbye to the dark cave and go out and see what it was like in the world beyond the curtain of vines.

So now the real problems would begin, I thought, and felt as apprehensive as the father. Now, more than ever, it seemed to me that it was essential to find a way to persuade the foxes to stay on the property. I suspected that they had lived before down by the bay and had come up to the cave on the ridge only to have their babies and now would return with them to their old territory. The field by the bay was nice, I could see that. It was about a mile long and several hundred yards wide, a pleasant curve of unspoiled shoreline on which there were two majestic stands of very tall and beautifully shaped Australian pines, thick clusters of seagrape and a fringe of mangrove along the water's edge. There were doves in the field, cover in the grass, and it must have been a good hunting ground for foxes. But down there the guns and the dogs were waiting.

Four   I am fallible. My judgment is not always good. I have done some very dumb things in my time.

For two days I restrained myself. On the third I went out and lowered a package of chicken necks into the cave. I knew that the kits and the mother fox were in the cave at the time because I had just seen her chase them in a few minutes before. They had been playing in the garden, racing around pellmell, and she had finally stood all she was going to stand of it. She had rounded them up like a sheep dog and chased them back into the cave, while the male had done his nervous little dance on his tiptoes up in the driveway. This had been going on for three days. The kits would burst out of the cave and dash about with complete abandon for as long as they could get away with it. Then they would get chased back to the cave and would be still until the next time they managed to escape, which would usually be pretty soon after. I wondered how they were getting anything to eat. When could the father and mother go hunting if they had to stand guard over the kits all the time? I assumed that the kits were still not weaned, or at least not entirely, so that took care of them, but how about the little mother? Foxes eat birds, fruit, insects, frogs, birds' eggs and rodents, but she looked as if she was existing on thin air.

The male looked just as bad, and I had plenty of chances to see him fairly close up now. Instead of hiding from me he showed himself all the time. He seemed to know that I had found out he had kits and that they were in the cave, and I imagined that he was trying to distract my attention from them by letting me see him. I had to walk along the driveway several times a day—mostly going to and from my car—and when I came to the point where the road passed over the cave he would come out of the bushes, glance at me to make sure that I had seen him, hesitate, duck back into the bushes and then reappear a little farther on ahead of me. He was being very brave, but I felt sorry for him because he seemed so uncertain about his role. I had the feeling that showing himself to me pained him terribly. It was his duty, but it was absolutely contrary to his nature.

Now, every time I walked along the driveway, I thought about all the times I had passed over the cave without ever guessing that the little foxes were down there. As a matter of fact, the branch of the tree on which I had found Chippy waiting for me that day after I had let her go stuck out almost directly above the cave, and the babies and the mother must have heard me, down there in the darkness, when I had spoken to her and asked her if she wanted to go home.

As I say, I restrained myself, because I was afraid that if I let on that I knew the kits were in the cave the mother would feel trapped and would take them away. So I tried at first to act as if I knew nothing and went about my business

33

121848

in my normal way, until I realized from the manner in which the father presented himself to me that they knew that I knew, and then I began to think, Well, things can't go on like this. I'm going to give them some chicken necks whether they like it or not. I'm not going to let them starve. I'll just hope that they'll sense that I'm only trying to help and will go ahead and gorge themselves.

I took a package of chicken necks out of the icebox and tied a long piece of string around it. Then I waited, watching at the window until I was sure that the mother and the kits were in the cave. Hurrying down the steps, I had misgivings, but I kept going. The male popped out of the bushes as usual when he heard me coming. I stopped and showed him the package, trying to think of some way to convey to him the assurance that it could not be in any way harmful to foxes. He gazed at me doubtfully, his nose high in the air. I understood that there was some danger in what I was about to do, but I was counting heavily on my feeling that the male knew that I was not an enemy. I don't mean that I believed he trusted me completely, only that he didn't think of me as an overt threat. He withdrew into the bushes and then reappeared as usual a little farther on. In the meantime I had gone over to the line of jagged coral rocks cemented together that formed a border along the edge of the driveway and, standing on one of the rocks, looked down into the garden. It was a rather heady experience. I was intensely aware that the mother and the kits were only a couple of feet below me and that they were probably waiting breathlessly to see what I was going to do.

I looked again at the male and saw that he had come back halfway toward me.

There was a ledge about a foot wide that curved across

the mouth of the cave. I lowered the package down to the ledge and let the string go. Without hesitating a moment I turned and walked quickly away.

I didn't look back once but went upstairs and ran to the windows overlooking the garden. From there I could see clearly the package of chicken necks on the ledge. They were just as I had left them. I brought a chair over to the windows and settled down to keep watch. The father fox was nowhere in sight now, and nothing stirred in the mouth of the cave.

Chippy had known from the beginning that I was up to something, and while I had been tying the string around the package she had begun running very fast in her cage, a sign of great excitement. I knew that she had observed me all the time I was outside. Now she lay on a branch with her nose sticking through the bars of her cage, also watching the cave.

Nothing happened.

I waited a long time, and then I got up and fiddled around for a while, coming back to the windows frequently to see if there was any action. But whereas I had been seeing the kits and the parents almost every time I had looked out the windows for the past two days, now the whole afternoon wore away without my seeing any of them, and the chicken necks stayed right where I had dropped them. Chippy had given up watching long ago. I gave up too and did some work.

Toward evening I couldn't stand it any longer and went outside. I didn't know exactly what I was going to do, but I wanted somehow to find out what had happened—why the foxes seemed suddenly to have disappeared.

At dusk it was a little eerie in the sunken garden. It was a wild and cheerful place on a sunny day, with the wind making the leaves dance and the squirrels playing and all the birds fluttering about and singing, but once the sun was down behind the trees it got very quiet in the garden. The darkness seemed to flow in there first and fill it up, and the vines hanging from the high branches took on a sinister look as the night birds began sailing through them. I could hear cars going past on the road at the rear of the property, but only faintly. High above the trees, where they were still touched by the sun, seagulls in great flights coasted swiftly across the sky, from west to east, returning from a day in the Everglades to their islands in the bay where they always spent the night.

I stood at the edge of the garden, near the steps that led down to the wellhouse. From there I had a close look at the mouth of the cave, but I couldn't see anything. I walked slowly around the garden and along the driveway, waiting for the male fox to show himself. Nothing moved except the lizards in the dry leaves at the edge of the driveway. I walked all the way around the garden and finally came back to the steps.

I had to push the vines aside to descend the steps, and I made a great commotion wading through the ferns and the vines on the ground as I made my way toward the cave. When I got there, something told me that the foxes were just not in the cave any more. So I parted the vines and looked in. The kits were gone and the mother was gone. All that remained was the package of chicken necks on the ledge.

I sat on a cement bench by the swimming pool and thought about what a serious mistake I had made. In effect, with my compulsive good-doing, I had chased the foxes out of their dry and secure den, the very last thing I had wanted to do, and I was sure they would never go back to it. It was October, still the rainy season, and I didn't know of any other place on the property where the foxes could find shelter.

The swimming pool was empty. In fact, I had filled it only once since I had lived there. Like the house, it was about fifty years old and therefore didn't have any of the modern conveniences, such as an automatic filtering system—or any filtering system. All you could do was fill it up and leave the water in until it started to turn green and then let it out, scrub the pool and fill it again, which was simply not worth the trouble. So I had filled it that once (a major operation in itself that had taken two days, because the pool filled from the well and you could run the pump for only half an hour at a time or it overheated), and I had had a good week or so of splashing and that had been that. But even though the pool was empty the deck around it was an excellent place to sun yourself or to sit in the evening and get the breeze. A balustrade enclosed the pool, with a massive bench on either side of the entrance. The balusters were cracking, revealing the rusty iron cores around which they had been cast. (The house also was reinforced with iron rods and it was cracking in several places too. In fact, all of the houses in the area that had been built of the same material and at about the same time were cracking. Like clockwork. Apparently it took exactly fifty years for the iron to expand to the point where it began to crack the concrete surrounding it.) On either side of the pool were basins in the shape of seashells. Poised above each basin was a devilish face, crudely sculptured out of cement, with a piece of rusty pipe sticking out of its mouth that spouted water in a thin stream if you turned a certain valve.

A cat was drowsing in one of the basins. Down at the deep

end of the pool another cat, a young one, was chasing the berries from the ficus tree as they fell. A gigantic ficus tree spread its branches out over the pool, and every year it produced thousands and thousands of small, hard black berries. In the evening the younger cats, and occasionally some of the more sporting-minded of the older ones, would gather in the pool and chase the berries as they fell and bounced and skittered down the sharply inclined floor of the pool. The game went on and on, and the berries kept accumulating at the deep end of the pool, where gradually they formed a mulch that clogged the drain. Then, when it rained, the pool would start to fill up, and if I let it go for a while the stagnant water would come alive with tadpoles, shooting around like atoms in a reactor, and when I finally waded into the water with a long pole to scrape the drain clear I would feel them nibbling at my ankles. The other end of the drain-pipe was halfway down the ridge, just a piece of six-inch pipe protruding from the earth, and it seemed that if I didn't check it for a couple of months it would get plugged up, with roots growing up into it, and I would have to pull them out, in one long rope, all braided tightly together, like a brown swollen ten- or fifteen-foot snake.

Everything grew so fast. And there never was an end to it. I couldn't console myself by saying, "Yes, but when winter comes it will all stop." It never stopped. Something was always flowering or bearing. When it was not one thing's time it was another's. The fall of leaves was staggering. I would have had to sweep day and night just to keep the driveway clear of leaves, never mind the rest of the place. The branches of the Florida holly tree are supposed to grow a foot a month. Woman's tongue is about as bad. Most of the trees never lost their leaves altogether but just kept dropping the old ones and getting new ones. I had my hands full cutting the grass, raking leaves and carrying the daily deadfall out to the trash pile by the road, and all the while the holly was creeping in from all sides. The open spaces seemed to get smaller and smaller every day.

The ficus beside the swimming pool was a big tree, and its great roots were steadily cracking the sides and the floor of the pool along with the rusting iron rods. But it wasn't the biggest ficus on the property. That distinction went to the one that towered over my house. It must have been well over a hundred feet tall, and it must have had a dozen limbs that were close to a hundred feet long. When I looked at it, out of my bedroom window, it was like looking up from the deck at the masts and rigging of a clipper ship. Each limb was a village of birds in itself, and the whole tree was a babbling city. From the limbs the new roots blew in the wind, like rough brown twine, reaching for the ground. When they finally touched the ground and took hold in it they quickly thickened and coiled themselves around the trunk and became part of the trunk, melting into it like wax. I couldn't help thinking now and then of what would happen if that tree came down in a hurricane. It would crush the house.

I almost always felt a cool breeze when I sat by the pool. It came up the slope from the bay, between the double row of royal palms that lined the driveway down in front. I could see the bay from where I sat, or at least a glimpse of it through the trees, where it turned dark blue out near the horizon.

I was enjoying the breeze, idly watching the cat, which had by now been joined by a couple of others, chase berries and thinking of how dumb I had been interfering with the foxes, when three things happened. First, one of the seed pods on the monkey dinner-bell tree exploded. The monkey dinner-bell tree was an exotic that had been imported from somewhere east of Suez by the original owner of the place. As I understood it, he had been in some way associated with Dr. David Grandison Fairchild, the botanist who had developed the famous Fairchild Tropical Garden in Miami, and had joined him in bringing in plants and trees and flowers from all over the world to experiment with in growing them in the United States. This accounted for the presence of the cannonball tree in the sunken garden and all of the other strange trees on the property. The monkey dinner-bell tree was frightening enough just as it stood, armed as it was on its trunk and limbs with murderous long thorns, but when the pods began exploding it was truly a menace. The pods were about the size of tangerines, and they were divided like tangerines into crescent-shaped sections. The sections were thin and brittle and each contained a flat seed about the size of a dime. The pods exploded at uncertain intervals like fragmentation grenades, throwing their sections every which way for thirty or forty feet. I never really got used to it. I would be walking along and suddenly hear a loud pop and then the pieces of the pod would fall like shrapnel around me. Usually I would have forgotten all about the monkey dinner-bell tree and would wonder what on earth was happening.

Anyway, this time no sooner had the pieces of the pod stopped pelting the driveway than I heard something moving behind me. I looked around and saw a big tom cat dragging the package of chicken necks up the steps from the sunken garden and across the lawn to the safety of some bushes nearby.

Then I had the unmistakable feeling of being stared at, and I looked back. There was the male fox, standing in the curve of the driveway, just where it closed the half circle around the swimming pool and started to dip down the slope. He was partly hidden by a skinny, almost leafless bougainvillaea bush that was heavy with flowers of a particularly vivid red (in general, the more parched and woebegone the bougainvillaea bush looks, the more abundant and impressive the flowers it produces). As usual, I didn't see him at first, even though I was looking right at him. But when I did see him I noticed immediately that he seemed terribly nervous, which, together with the fact that he had shown himself to me at all, I took to mean that the kits were somewhere close by. Then, back in the dark shadows near the base of the monkey dinner-bell tree, I heard a crashing about in the underbrush and saw flashes of swift movement, and I knew the kits were at their games.

The mother came out of the shadows and stood about halfway between the male and the kits. I sat gazing at them and they stood gazing at me, and there we were all back together again.

Then, as mysteriously as he had come, the male turned and disappeared around the side of the pool, down the slope. At that, the female moved back into the shadows. Since the kits had abruptly stopped their playing, a silence fell, broken only by the hum of the wings of the low-flying night birds, the patter of the berries falling and the soft-footed scampering of the cats in the pool.

The stars had come out. It was almost dark. I could see the blinking lights of the channel markers in the bay.

I should have returned to the house then and prepared my simple evening meal and gone back to work on my novel and forgotten all about the foxes for the moment. Instead, I fell once more under the irresistible spell of my compulsion to provide food for the foxes whether they liked it or not. I marched upstairs and got a half dozen eggs out of the refrigerator, put them in a bowl and went back out to the place where I had seen the little foxes.

It was spooky back there, day or night. There was a strange pond under the trees that was always full of dark water where the wild animals from all around came to drink. There was the monkey dinner-bell tree with its awful thorns, a royal poinciana with huge pods hanging down from its bare branches like long leather tongues and a hibiscus with peach-colored flowers that had grown to an incredible height, trying to reach up for sunlight through the dense foliage above it. In the middle of it all was a pile of large rocks, built up like a well around a shaft that went straight down into the ground. The shaft was natural and was about twenty feet deep. The story was that the pirate Black Caesar had buried his treasure in the tunnel that ran from the bottom of the shaft all the way back to the base of another shaft a couple of hundred feet away, close to the wall at the rear of the property. I don't know how much truth there was in the story, but it was established that Black Caesar had operated out of the bay, and I knew a man who had found some English and Spanish coins dating from the right period on the ground near the mouth of the shaft. But he also said that he had gone through the tunnel from end to end once and hadn't found a thing.

I had decided on eggs because I knew that foxes liked them and cats didn't. I placed the eggs carefully around the pond in an arrangement that I thought would be attractive and appetizing to foxes, and then I hurried home.

The next morning when I went to check on the eggs I observed from a slight distance that they were all still there. However, a little later I happened to come along the driveway and saw the little father just disappearing around the swimming pool, on his way down the slope, carrying an egg in his mouth.

It was a beautiful moment of triumph for me. I felt that at last I had communicated with the foxes.

Five   IN LATE October, which is about the time when the merciless humidity and the stunning heat that persist in southeast Florida for most of the year finally relent, I began to work on the terrace in the afternoons, which meant that Chippy could come down with me and visit with her friends.

Carrying her in her cage down to the terrace was a risky venture because she could escape from the bottom. Not that she wanted to. It was just her curiosity. She might see a leaf on the steps that she would like to have, or a fern growing out of the rocks that looked worth investigating. It was difficult to watch her and see where I was going at the same time. I was afraid of stepping on her or crushing her with the bottom rim of the cage, of losing my balance and cartwheeling down the steps. The simple solution would be to clip a sheet of newspaper across the bottom of the cage with clothespins, but usually I was too lazy. I just picked up the cage and took my chances. Once in a while Chippy would actually hop down onto the steps when I was carrying her either up or down, and then I would stand there holding the heavy cage up, quivering all over, my eyes popping, waiting until she finally took the leaf or whatever it was in her mouth and climbed back in. It never seemed to occur to her to slip out from under the cage, but that was because she wasn't concentrating on freedom but on the thing that had caught her eye in the first place.

The terrace was small, with a balustrade around it, and it was paved with flat coral rocks with deep crevices between them, in which there was soil and grass grew. At one end there were the steps leading up to my front door, the trellis covered with bougainvillaea and the steps going down to the ground. At the other end there was a big old-fashioned white-painted iron glider that was supposed to have been acquired from the grand old Royal Palm Hotel in Miami when it had been condemned as unsound in 1930 and all of its furniture and fixtures had been auctioned off, prior to clearing the land to make way for a parking lot (which survives to this day). The glider had handsome dark-blue cushions with white piping, and when I sat on it, gliding sedately back and forth at the flick of my heel, I could easily imagine myself on the verandah of the Royal Palm, watching all the tones in Panama hats and long dresses promenading about in the formal gardens.

I always put Chippy's cage exactly in the middle of the terrace. The reason for this was that on all sides my collection of ferns was closing in, and since I had found most of the specimens in the depths of the Everglades and didn't even know the names of some of them, I was afraid to let her nibble the leaves, thinking they might be poisonous. She wanted badly to get at them. She would cling to the bars of her cage, her nose stuck through the bars, and reach her hand out toward them as far as it would go, futilely clawing the air. About this time I had read a book called *Out of the Woods,* in which the author had told how she had raised three fox squirrels from infancy and how her favorite of the three had died suddenly after she had given him a flower from her garden to eat. She was convinced that squirrels don't know by instinct which plants are poisonous to them but are taught by their mothers what to look out for; therefore, when they have been raised by people they cannot be trusted to know what's good for them. This had made a deep impression on me, and whether it was necessarily so or not, I had resolved not to take any chances. If I hadn't actually seen one of the wild squirrels on the property eat something, I wouldn't let my squirrel have it.

One of Chippy's greatest pleasures in life was digging up sunflower seeds out of the grass on the terrace that she had buried there the last time I had brought her down. She worked very hard at burying them, digging down with her claws in the earth and rooting with her long nose until her face was in the hole right up to the eyes. An enormous amount of snuffling and snorting accompanied the digging, and when she had finally dropped the seed into the hole and covered it with dirt and bits of grass and stray leaves, her nose was black. For a moment she would look pleased with herself, and then she would dig up the seed and bury it somewhere else.

Why?

You never knew, and that was why you couldn't watch her burying seeds for any length of time. If you did, it would drive you out of your clock. You would have a tremendous urge to impose your own logic on the situation, to ask a lot of questions, to demand to know why one place was better than another, or worse than another, to get down on your hands and knees and dig with her and snuffle in the earth. (It was worse in the house, of course, where there wasn't any dirt or bits of grass or leaves but where she went through all the motions of burying and hiding anyway.)

I think there must have been something genuinely intoxicating to her about the seeds that she dug up out of the earth after they had been buried for a couple of days. Was it the smell? Was it the fact that she had found something hidden, even if she had hidden it herself? Did she kid herself that she had found the cache of another squirrel? Whatever it was, there was a feverishness about the way she would turn the seed over and over in her hands, sniffing at it very fast, in the squirrel's way, that always reminded me of the misers in the old movies when they went into their secret chests and took out a jewel or a gold coin and fondled it. The difference was that they didn't end up by wolfing down their treasures, and Chippy did.

When I sat on the glider in the afternoons, writing in my notebooks, sooner or later I would begin to feel surrounded. I would look up finally and glance about, carefully, not too quickly, and I would see that the birds had gathered silently all around the terrace. They were in the pine tree, in the jasmine, on the roof of the house, on the telephone wires, on the long arms of the oak, in the bougainvillaea—blue jays, cardinals, mockingbirds, sparrows, wrens, cat birds, red-bellied woodpeckers, spotted-breasted orioles and painted buntings. They came because they knew that when Chippy was down on the terrace I was more generous than usual in putting out food for them. (They were all addicted to powdered-sugar doughnuts, which I crumbled up for them several times a day on the window ledge overlooking the terrace.) So I would go and get a couple of doughnuts and a

bag of sunflower seeds. The doughnuts I put on the window ledge as usual, but the seeds I put on the ground all around the bottom of the cage, where Chippy could get them but the birds could get them too. When I sat down again on the glider the birds moved in. All of them except the cardinals and the blue jays went to the window ledge. The cardinals and the blue jays liked doughnuts as well as the next bird, but generally speaking they preferred sunflower seeds if they had a choice in the matter.

I must say that Chippy was not a bad little hostess. She didn't run at the birds or try to beat them up when they took her seeds. As long as she got her share she seemed to think it was okay for them to get theirs. She watched them closely and in fact I think she truly enjoyed the company of the birds. All except the male cardinals. Their bright red made her a little uneasy, and she didn't much like the *tick-tick-tick* sound they made when they were hopping around on the terrace near her cage. When she was inside the house and that sound came near her, it occasionally set her to scolding vehemently. I don't know why it never bothered her that much when she was outside, but it's possible that she was afraid to scold when she wasn't in the house, feeling that she was too vulnerable.

There was a good deal going on then, with the birds landing and taking off from the ledge, squabbling among themselves, fluttering down to steal seeds from Chippy, and Chippy herself burying fresh seeds and digging up old ones. After a while the bathing would begin. There was a bird-bath on the terrace, and when two or three birds started splashing in it together the water would fly as far as the cage, upsetting Chippy, who didn't know what it was to bathe and didn't want to learn.

√

I enjoyed watching Chippy with her friends, but now and then I couldn't help wondering if I wasn't a little too much like the rich father with the unpopular child who has to bribe the neighborhood kids with candy and prizes to come over and play with his kid.

Anyway, sooner or later the squirrels would arrive like a gang of toughs to break up the party. They were just as hopelessly addicted to powdered-sugar doughnuts as everybody else, if not more so. Three or four of them would leap over from the peanut-butter tree to the balcony outside my front door. From there they would run onto the top of the trellis and lurk under the bougainvillaea for a minute, looking the situation over. Then one of them would jump to the ledge and scatter the birds, and then they would all jump over and eat the remaining crumbs. I had tried many times to discourage them from coming to the ledge. Not that I minded them eating the doughnuts. I was afraid that one of them would get caught by a cat. Squirrels are quite uncatchable by anything when they are in the trees, but out of the trees an alert cat can get them if they're not careful. My latest technique was the peanut-butter tree, which was actually the sapodilla tree that grew near my balcony. I had been pasting gobs of peanut butter to one of the limbs, hoping that the squirrels would stuff themselves so thoroughly on that that they wouldn't have any room left for doughnuts. I did the pasting at great personal danger to myself by means of a curtain rod that I kept beside the door for that specific purpose. I would bring out a jar of peanut butter, dig out a gob with a knife, paste it onto the curtain rod and then lean far out and paste it onto the limb of the tree. I had to lean out a long way, and I could have fallen and broken my neck doing it. But the peanut butter didn't keep the squirrels from coming to the ledge. They liked the peanut butter just fine, and not only did they lap it all up but also chewed away the bark where it had been. However, they always seemed to leave room for crumbled doughnuts.

Chippy didn't pay much attention to the wild squirrels, and they ignored her. The only time they had anything to do with each other was when one of them would come over to the cage and steal some seeds. Chippy tolerated the birds, but the squirrels were another matter. She would run at them and try to scare them away, and if that didn't work she would run up and cling upside down to the screen across the top of her cage and start squealing as if she was being murdered. In the end, I usually had to chase the squirrels away from the terrace. When they were back in the peanut-butter tree I would drop some pieces of doughnut to the ground at the base of the tree where they could run down and get them, to show them that I still liked them even if they were rather a pain sometimes.

It had always been a secret wish of mine that Chippy would strike up a friendship with one of the wild squirrels and that, whenever she was on the terrace, her friend would come and see her. She would share her things with him or her, and they would play and romp and rub noses through the bars of her cage, or whatever. Well, all right, what I really wished was that Chippy and a wild squirrel would get to be such great pals that eventually we might even be able to invite the squirrel to come into the house with us. Then the two of them could tussle and chase each other and play marvelous games together. What I'm saying is that I would have gone a long way toward helping a happy relationship to get rolling and once it was rolling to keep it rolling, but it never happened. And it never happened because the wild squirrels never gave it a chance. Not one of them ever made the slightest effort to get to know Chippy. After all, it was up to them to go to her, not the other way around, I think, inasmuch as they were free and could go to her but she certainly couldn't go to them. All it would have required from them was a little patience and understanding. Yes, she got excited and perhaps even a little hysterical whenever they came anywhere near her cage, but she was just a young girl squirrel without much experience of anything, whereas they were worldly and knew all the answers and should have been able to make allowances for things. She was a very nice squirrel. She had lovely eyes and a sweet expression and one of the biggest, bushiest and most beautiful tails I've ever seen. So what was wrong with them? Why couldn't they have made an effort? It wouldn't have killed them. Their trouble was that they didn't know a wonderful little soul crying out for friendship when they saw one, and they couldn't have cared less anyway. All they were even faintly interested in was sunflower seeds and doughnuts and peanut butter. They had no sensitivity. No kindness. No manners. No culture. No class. No nothing!

I'm sorry. I seem to have gotten a little bit carried away. But you know what I mean.

Six ONE MORNING I was awakened quite early by the barking of the foxes. I knew that they must be right below my living-room windows because I could hear them so clearly, and I knew it was the foxes because nothing else living that I know of makes a noise like that. It's a very dry, rasping bark and, frankly, an unpleasant sound. It reminded me of when I was a deckhand once on a yacht that spent most of its time on the French Riviera. The owners had a papier-mâché bulldog with a big spiked collar around its neck that was kept on the stern near the gangway when we were in Cannes. It was so lifelike that when children saw it they would laugh and point and dance around on the quai, thinking it was real. The owner would pull the chain that was attached to the dog's collar, and it would bark. The foxes' bark always reminded me of that toy dog on the stern of the *Vagrant*, because his bark was the only one I had ever heard that sounded just like theirs.

The barking stopped and I started to go back to sleep, but then it began again. I lay awake trying to decide whether to get up and see what was going on or stay where I was and let whatever it was run its course.

Ever since the foxes had finally decided to take the eggs from me, I had been in fairly close touch with them. I would catch a glimpse of the kits dashing madly around in the bushes about once a day, and of course whenever I saw them the parents were always present too. I had been delivering eggs and packages of chicken necks to them regularly at our tacitly agreed-on drop near the pond under the monkey dinner-bell tree, and they had been taking them fairly regularly too. But they were foxes, and so there were days when they wouldn't touch a thing, and on those days, sooner or later, one of the cats would venture over and make off with the chicken.

The relationship between the foxes and the cats was roughly comparable to that of Germany and France in the period 1914–1918. One morning after I had put out some chicken necks I stood for a minute, as was my custom, near the pond, making the clicking noises with my tongue against the roof of my mouth that I used to call the foxes, and then I sat down on a bench by the pool to watch for them. I knew that they could pick up my call no matter where they were on the property, even though it wasn't very loud. The problem was that the cats knew that call too and knew what it meant. Half a dozen of them were sprawled in the shade in the driveway at the time, and one of them got up and ambled around the far end of the pool. He was acting as if he didn't have a thing on his mind, but I knew where he was going. I saw him appear around the other side of the pool a moment later. He was just moping along, stopping to sniff a blade of grass now and then, the way cats will, and to sit down and give himself an occasional scratch behind the ear.

He seemed to be wandering aimlessly in the sunshine, but I could see very clearly that he was working his way slowly but surely toward the chicken necks. Finally, he paused to sniff a fern and then disappeared into the bushes. For two or three seconds nothing happened, and then the cat came out of the bushes and shot past me, breaking all previous land speed records for cats and closely followed by the male fox, who didn't even have it out of second gear but was just cruising along, nipping at the cat's tail.

This cat, an orange-and-white specimen with amber eyes, was top cat in the neighborhood, and to prove it he would give one of the other males a good sound drubbing whenever the mood was on him, which was just about all the time. For some reason the male fox felt compelled to make an appearance at the scene every time there was a cat fight. I would hear the familiar wailing and howling begin and look out the window, and in a moment without fail there the fox would be, with his anxious look, adding his rasping bark to the din. I guess he considered any sort of disturbance a potential threat to his babies and felt that he had to keep an eye on the situation.

The barking continued, and I realized that I would have to go out to see what it was all about. In the first place, it wasn't only the male fox this time. It sounded like several foxes. And there wasn't a cat fight going on as far as I could hear.

I went to the living room and looked first at Chippy's cage, as I always did when something was happening outside and I wanted a quick appraisal. She was looking out of her window and her tail was twirling, which meant that she was alarmed.

I joined her at her window and saw a very strange sight.

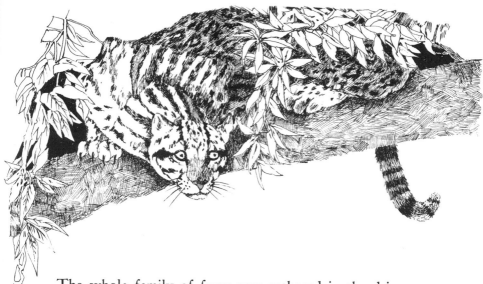

The whole family of foxes was gathered in the driveway, the mother and father in the front rank and the three kits right behind them, and they were all barking at something that was, apparently, in the big mango tree that stood at the edge of the sunken garden. I moved back and forth from window to window, but I couldn't see the lower part of the mango tree because of some foliage that was in the way.

I put on some clothes and went outside, and when I was halfway down the steps I froze. I could see the whole mango tree from there, and crouching on a low limb was a large yellow cat with black spots that looked to me like either a leopard or a jaguar. It was a breathtaking experience to see him there, and my first impulse was to turn right around and go back upstairs and lock myself in. But my curiosity got the better of me, and I went down the steps and walked slowly toward the tree. I was so fascinated by the cat that I didn't even think about the foxes, and then I found myself right in the midst of them. They milled around me, barking and growling, moving in on the cat and darting back. When one of them brushed against my leg I did take a moment to reflect on the irony of the fact that they had taken so much trouble to elude me for such a long time and now here they were treating me like one of the gang.

The cat snarled back at the foxes, displaying impressive fangs, and struck at them when they got close, letting them see his lethal claws. He looked to be about three times the size of the male fox, and I thought that if he decided to come down and tangle with him he would make short work of the fox, or, for that matter, the whole family of them and me too.

I truly couldn't imagine what I should do next. The scene was so peculiar—a family of foxes holding a jungle cat at bay—that it bewildered me. I kept thinking that I ought to go call somebody. But I couldn't think who. And what would I have said anyway?

All of a sudden the cat jumped to the ground and threw the foxes and me into a panic. We stumbled all over each other falling back, and I know that if I had had a tail I would

have put it between my legs too, as they did. The cat landed in a patch of snake plants, paused there for a moment, gazing at us in our abject confusion, and then he laid his ears flat, opened his mouth wide to give us another sensational view of his fangs, lashed his great tail a couple of times, coughed hollowly like the lions in the zoo and finally turned and loped off along the driveway toward my house.

The minute the cat's back was turned the foxes regained their courage and trotted after him, and I went with them, swept up in the spirit of the chase. A handful of blue jays accompanied us, crying frantically and swooping back and forth above the cat. I couldn't help noticing in passing that the group of tabby cats that normally would have been lounging below my windows at this time apparently had left town.

The cat went to the west end of the house, turned the corner and, without hesitating, ran lightly up the long flight of wooden steps to the landing outside my back door. The steps were very steep. In fact, they seemed to go almost straight up. The landing had a railing around it and a slanted roof overhead. When he reached the landing the cat bounded up onto the railing and sat there, staring down at us.

It was at that point that my compulsion to take care of animals whether they liked it or not (which had already, as we have seen, gotten me into trouble with the foxes) took control of me again. It seemed to me that the cat looked terribly thirsty. I don't know what made me think so. His tongue wasn't hanging out. Anyway, I felt that I had to give him some water.

So I hurried around to the front steps and ran upstairs. In the kitchen I got a big mixing bowl and filled it with water. On my way back through the living room I saw Chippy standing on her hind legs on a branch, grasping the bars of her cage with her hands and rocking her head excitedly back and forth, which meant that she was dying to be let out. But I had no time for squirrels.

When I returned to the back steps with the water I saw that the mother fox and the kits had disappeared. Only the male fox and the cat watched my slow ascent of the steps. When I was about halfway up I began to have vague misgivings about the wisdom of what I was doing, but it wasn't until I was three steps from the top that it really struck home to me that I was doing something that everybody knows you shouldn't do—put a dangerous animal in a corner.

I stopped and looked at the cat. He didn't twitch a muscle but gazed straight into my eyes. I was, of course, very close to him then, and he was a beautiful thing. I spoke to him softly, saying something inane but hoping that from the tone of my voice he would know that I had come in friendship. He undulated slightly, as if he was setting himself to do something, and suddenly I was terrified. My heart started pounding. I was covered with sweat, and the hair on my arms and the back of my neck crawled. Besides that, I felt weak all over. For a person who is one of the world's truly great natural cowards, it was a tough spot to be in.

I was standing with my back to the wall of the house, and I was afraid to do anything. Running away was out of the question. I was certain that the instant my back was turned the cat would spring. I couldn't even lean down and put the bowl of water on the landing, which had been my intention. I was holding the bowl in my right hand and it had begun to quiver, but I was afraid to put the bowl down because I thought the cat might consider it an aggressive action. The bowl was made of stainless steel, and as it quivered in my hand it caught the sunlight. I was afraid that all this quivering and glittering in my hand might get the cat excited, so I carefully raised my left hand and made it grip the bowl too. Then I gradually drew the bowl in toward me so that I could brace it against my stomach. This stopped the quivering, but the bowl wasn't level, and water spilled over onto my shirt and ran down the front of my pants and dripped on the steps. I didn't care. I remembered those stories that you come across in the papers now and then about the lion tamer who goes into the cage once too often and the next thing you know it's a hundred and twenty-seven stitches. I was thinking, "This is the tenth of November 1966, and something awful is going to happen to me."

Abruptly, the cat jumped down onto the landing, and without even thinking about what I was doing I put the bowl of water in front of him. Perhaps it was simply a desperate effort to get something between him and me. In any event, I had finally done what I had come up the steps to do, and the cat came over and drank the water with his long pink tongue.

When he had drunk about half the bowl the cat stopped drinking and looked up at me. Then he moved toward me. My right hand was hanging limply at my side. The cat took the wrist in his wet mouth and closed his fangs on it gently, with about the same amount of pressure as a nurse taking your pulse.

Then he glided past me and down the steps, and the fox made way for him. He loped around the west side of the sunken garden, with the fox following at a discreet distance. I ran down the steps and fell in behind the fox, and I caught a glimpse of the cat just before he disappeared into the tall grass in the broad field between the driveway and the line of oaks at the south end of the property.

I stopped, and the fox paused and looked back at me,

standing in the sunlight. When he saw that I wasn't coming any farther he seemed to lose his enthusiasm for the hunt. We kept looking at each other and hesitating, and finally he trotted across the driveway and melted into the dark shade under the trees, heading toward his new territory down by the monkey dinner-bell tree.

I went upstairs and called the police department and asked if they knew anything about a big cat that might have escaped from somewhere.

"When you say big, how big do you mean?" the officer asked.

"About thirty pounds," I said. "Yellow with black spots. I think he's either a leopard, a jaguar or an ocelot."

"And he's on the premises right now?"

"Yes, he is," I said.

"Have you got a gun?" he asked.

"No, I don't," I said.

"Well, you stay in the house then," he said, "and I'll send a man with a rifle down there directly to take care of the problem for you. Now what's your name and address?"

I hung up. It seemed to me that there had to be some way of taking care of the problem short of slaughtering the animal. So I called the Humane Society, and they said they would send a man down who would try to catch the animal alive.

The instant I gave them my name and address I bit my tongue. By law I wasn't supposed to have a squirrel. So I hurriedly picked up Chippy's cage and moved her away from her window overlooking the driveway and the sunken garden and put her in the bedroom.

It took about an hour for the man from the Humane Society to put in an appearance. I spent the time going around to the neighbors and asking them if they had seen the cat. They all looked at me in a funny way. The Humane Society man also looked at me in a funny way, but he got a dog collar and a leash out of his truck and asked me to show him where I had last seen the animal.

I took him to the place, and he stood there gazing at the field, squinting in the sunlight and fiddling with the leash.

"He could be in Chicago by now," he said.

"That's right," I said.

Then I couldn't resist any longer, and I came right out and asked him if he really thought the cat was going to let him walk up and put that collar around his neck.

He looked at me in a funny way again. "I don't know," he said. "He might."

I left him to his own devices and went over and sat on a bench in front of the house to observe the great hunt. The man ambled into the field and stood there smoking a cigarette for a while. Then he returned and walked along the driveway toward the swimming pool. I was positive that the foxes were watching him too from back in the trees. I could see a couple of squirrels looking down at him from an oak in the sunken garden. He went around the pool and walked on down the slope, and then he came back in a few minutes and said that he couldn't seem to find the cat anywhere. He got some forms out of his truck and asked me to sign a release stating that he had come to my address and investigated the situation with negative results. Then he said that there was of course no charge for his services but that if I wanted to make a voluntary contribution to the Humane Society to help defray the operating expenses of that organization, I should feel free to do so. So I gave him a couple of dollars and he gave me a receipt and went cheerfully on his way.

After that I drove down to the village and visited the local veterinarian. He said that he thought the cat was probably an ocelot. He knew several people who owned them but hadn't heard so far of any of them missing one. He gave me the phone number of a woman named Mrs. Sears, who, he said, was the president of the ocelot club, and he assured me that it anyone would know something about a missing ocelot it would be Mrs. Sears.

I went home and called Mrs. Sears, who thanked God from the bottom of her heart that I had found my way to her. She told me briefly what it was like being an ocelot owner, about the heartaches and the hassles they had to endure. It wasn't legal to own an ocelot, she explained, any more than it was legal to own a lion or a tiger, and the rigmarole you had to go through was so involved if you wanted to get a permit that most people just gave up and lived with their pets, as it were, in sin. This being the case, she went on, the worst thing that could happen to the club members was for one of their cats to run away, because then people started calling the police about the big cat they had seen prowling in the neighborhood, and sometimes the animal would get shot and sometimes trapped and never returned to its owner and always the incident precipitated a new round of trouble for the club members with the authorities.

Anyway, she told me that she would make a few calls and that very shortly some of the club members would come to my place and try to find the cat. She was as good as her word, for within an hour half a dozen men had gathered in my driveway to begin the search. They were all ocelot owners, and they had all dutifully dropped whatever they had been doing when they had gotten the call from Mrs.

Sears. (One of them was a garage mechanic who had been caught in the middle of a ring job on a truck and was covered with grease from head to foot.)

I went with them, and we fanned out in the field. Soon we came upon a circular place near an old rock garden where the grass had been beaten down, and the ocelot men agreed that that was where the cat must have made a nest by turning around and around before settling down.

Right after we made this discovery another member of the club arrived with the news that he had just been told by Mrs. Sears that Mary So-and-So had just called her to say that her male ocelot, Boujii, who had been missing for two days, had finally come home. Mary So-and-So didn't live very far away. It was logical to assume that the cat I had seen was Boujii. I went over to Mary's house with the club members, and she led us into the bedroom. It was the only room in the house that was air-conditioned, and back in the dark cool closet Boujii was curled up luxuriously. He raised his head and looked at me when Mary turned the light on. I recognized him, and I knew that he recognized me.

That evening I went out to the monkey dinner-bell tree with some eggs and clicked for the foxes, and after a while I saw the male far off down the slope gazing at me warily. That morning we had been two residents of the same territory allied against an intruder. Now we were simply fox and man again.

Seven   So THERE was an ocelot club. For all I knew there also could have been lion clubs, tiger clubs and even giraffe clubs. But one thing was certain: There were no squirrel clubs—with members who were ready to pitch in at a moment's notice and help out whenever there was a squirrel in trouble.

In December the thing I had always dreaded happened. Chippy got sick. But sick isn't really the word. Her vagina became swollen. I noticed it one day because the area around the base of a squirrel's tail is so thickly furred that on a female the vagina is normally almost completely hidden. I kept noticing it, and I began to worry. Something clearly was wrong.

At first I hoped that it was just a cyclical thing that would soon disappear by itself, but when I talked to the veterinarian in the village he said he didn't think so. He told me that if I wanted to bring Chippy in he would look at her— but there was the old problem again. I couldn't take Chippy to him because I couldn't take her anywhere, and even if he had been willing to make a house call she wouldn't have let him touch her, much less examine her. When I explained all that to the doctor he told me quite frankly that he didn't expect he would have been able to do much for my squirrel anyway. Everything about wild animals, he said, was so different from dogs and cats and all of the regular run of his patients that he considered them to be about as far out of his realm as jet engines.

A couple of weeks went by, and the swelling didn't go away. In fact, it got slightly worse. It looked about like the tip of my little finger standing up out of the surrounding white fur, pink and shiny, and it depressed me. Every morning I would go out and look at Chippy in her cage, hoping that the swelling would have miraculously disappeared overnight. In order to see anything I had to catch Chippy when she was balanced on one of her branches, sneak up on her, stoop over sideways, crane my neck around and look upward. It seemed to embarrass Chippy, and I think she thought I was definitely a bit queer. She would quickly reverse her position on the branch, and I would have to go around to the other side of the cage and try again. When I finally achieved my purpose the swelling was always still there. And, worst of all, every once in a while I would see Chippy pause in whatever she was doing and fuss at the swelling with her long, sharp lower teeth, and I knew that it bothered her.

I kept going to veterinarians, hoping against hope that I would find one eventually who would know what Chippy's problem was just from my description of it. He would know exactly what to tell me to do for it, and it would be a simple remedy that would get rid of the swelling in nothing flat. But I had no such luck. They all said more or less the same thing as the first man, and every day I felt more depressed and more convinced that pretty soon the situation was going to get very serious.

I was right.

One black morning I found Chippy fussing with herself continuously, and when in desperation I reached into her cage and tried to make her stop, she gave me a bite on the thumb that went right to the bone. I realized that the damned swelling, whatever it was, was probably driving her crazy.

Everything went wrong after that. I had an appointment on the other side of town that morning. I thought that my appointment wouldn't take long and that I would be able to come back soon and try to do something for Chippy. But when I was halfway there my car suddenly stopped. Or, rather, it just seemed to die, and I coasted over to the curb and sat there wondering what I was going to do next. Finally, I walked to a gas station down the road, and an attendant drove me back in his truck and made a quick diagnosis of my car's problem. It was very bad, he said. The timing gear was busted. I didn't really know what that meant, but I knew that I had had it. The gas-station man said that he was sorry but he couldn't help me, that I would have to have my car towed to a garage where they handled major work like that. Then he left me.

I sat on the fender of my car for a while in a state of the darkest despair, and then I left the car where it stood and walked many blocks in the other direction to a used-car lot that was owned by a friend of mine. I told him about my car and about my squirrel, and he took pity on me and lent me one of what he called his "junkers." The car was full of strange noises when it was just standing still with the engine running. When I actually started out down the road the noises increased to the point where everybody I passed stared at me, and pedestrians scurried to get out of my way, even though I wasn't going very fast. I couldn't go very fast. I also couldn't stop very fast. But luckily the air-conditioning worked. It was a blistering hot day, December or no December.

I forgot about my appointment and went straight home, and when I got there I found that, as I had feared would happen sooner or later, Chippy, in her frustration, had begun to scrape at the swelling with her sharp teeth, and there was blood on her fur.

I went outside and found a piece of heavy wire mesh and cut out a square roughly the size of the entrance to Chippy's house. I took it with me back into the house and put on a pair of thick pigskin gloves. Chippy was afraid of those gloves for some reason, and when she saw me approaching her cage she did what she always did when she saw me with them on. She ran up to her house and pulled her tail across the entrance and observed me through one of her little windows.

That was what I had counted on her doing, and I quickly opened her cage and tied the wire mesh across the front of her house, locking her in. It was the first time that I had ever trapped Chippy in her house, and the minute she realized that she was truly trapped she began biting desperately at the wire and scratching at it with her claws, turning around and around in her house, trying to find a way out.

Next, I stood on a chair and took the screen off the top of the cage and cut the strings that fastened Chippy's house to the underside of the uppermost branch in the cage. Then I lifted the house out of the cage, climbed down off the chair, put the house momentarily on the living-room table, removed my gloves, picked up the house again (which almost felt alive itself with the squirrel moving around inside it), went out the door, locking it behind me, and hurried down the steps and along the driveway to my car.

It was a big day of firsts for Chippy. It was the first time she had ever been trapped inside her house, the first time she had ever been carried around in her house and the first time she had ever been in a car.

I put the little house on the seat next to me in the car and started up the engine. The noise subdued Chippy. She lay flat on her stomach and kept perfectly still while I drove out through the gate and onto the road. Obviously, she was wondering what on earth could happen next to a squirrel. I turned on the air-conditioning, which cut down on the engine noise a little; but the blast of cold air revived Chippy, and she went back frantically to trying to get out of her house again.

I knew where I was going, but I hadn't the faintest idea what was going to happen when I got there. It was going to the zoo in a nearby city to see Dr. Harrison, who was the head veterinarian there. I had first heard of him in a newspaper article in which he had been called "the lion doctor" and had been described as having a miraculous way with wild animals. He was the man I had phoned as a last resort when Chippy had fallen on her head as a young squirrel. I had never met the man or spoken to him again after that day, and I wasn't even sure that he would still be at the zoo. But I had to do something, and this was the only thing left.

In order to reach the zoo I had to drive on a main highway, which meant cars whistling past in both directions and plenty of big trucks with air horns and air brakes. In an attempt to calm the squirrel during the ordeal, I stuck the tip of the middle finger of my right hand through an opening in the wire mesh and let her nibble on that instead of the wire. That did seem to calm her a little, but it also forced me to drive with one hand. Besides that I found myself taking all sorts of liberties with red lights and stop signs. In fact, it was one of those reckless rides on which you're always imagining yourself trying to explain things to a cop. ("The reason I'm breaking every law in the books, Officer, is that I'm taking my squirrel to the lion doctor to see if he can cure her of a problem of such a personal nature that I wouldn't discuss it with you if you locked me up for a thousand years.")

After I got off the highway I had to cross a bay and go over bridges and causeways, and I was very glad that Chippy couldn't see all that water down below us because I didn't think she would have understood about that.

By this time my left thumb (which Chippy had bitten earlier) had stopped being numb and was beginning to hurt badly. On top of that I had a splitting headache from the strain of the general situation, plus the fact that I hadn't had anything to eat so far that day except a cup of coffee. And the reality of what I was doing had begun to sink in as well. I had no right to bring my squirrel to the lion doctor without even telling him I was coming. He would certainly resent the hell out of it, if he was there at all. Which he probably wouldn't be. In other words, I was going a long way and wasting a lot of time for nothing.

I came to the main entrance to the zoo and asked some workmen where I might find the head veterinarian. They directed me along a back road that wound through a dense grove of coconut palms, and at the end of the road was a group of low buildings. I parked in front of the building that said "Office" and left Chippy in the car with the engine and the air-conditioning running and went inside.

I told my troubles to the girl at the desk. She seemed very understanding and told me that although Dr. Harrison wasn't in his office at the moment she expected him back shortly. She pointed out the doctor's office to me through the window and told me to take my squirrel and wait there. She said that she felt sure the doctor would at least look at Chippy and advise me about what could be done for her.

I left my car where it was and walked in the blazing sun to the doctor's office, carrying Chippy in her house in front of me with one finger stuck through the wire mesh. I went inside and sat in the outer office. There were three people in the office. Although I wanted to tell someone who I was and what I was doing there, none of them seemed even vaguely interested. It was as if fifty total strangers walked in every day carrying squirrels in boxes. A girl was very busy at a typewriter, a man in a zoo attendant's uniform was sitting behind a desk to my left and a portly man in a black suit and a white hat with a big cigar in his mouth sat in the chair to my right. The man with the cigar was talking animatedly to the zoo attendant, and it was clear from their conversation that he was the director of a small zoo in Upstate New York who was traveling around that winter looking over some of the larger zoos in the country.

As he talked the smoke came out of him in thick blue clouds that weren't carried away by the inadequate air-conditioning but only drifted languidly back and forth in front of him, me, and Chippy in her house in my lap. I could almost hear her choking on the foul air. I looked down at her and saw a trace of blood in the groove between her two lower teeth, which meant that she had loosened her teeth gnawing on the wire mesh. My headache got so bad that I could barely see straight.

Every once in a while one of the peacocks that I had seen wandering around freely outside let go a heart-stopping screech, and there was a steady background din of roaring and coughing from cages somewhere close to the rear of the building. For some reason it reminded me of a poem written by my sister at a very early age and carefully preserved by my mother. The poem was called "The Jungle" and went:

> The jungle is a tarrible place,
> A tarrible place is he.
> With lions roaring all around,
> I'd be a little scared,
> Don't you?

I waited a long time for the doctor. Maybe it was only twenty minutes. In any case, he finally came in and looked at me with my box and asked me to bring my squirrel into his office. The girl in the other office had told him about me, he said, and he added that he remembered very well our telephone conversation of about a year before.

He was a small man with a low voice and strong hands and forearms and very steady eyes. He looked about thirty-five. I could easily imagine him removing a thorn from a lion's paw. I put Chippy's house on his desk, and he smiled at her. He seemed what I had hoped to God he would be—a kind man.

"Look," he said, "I'm not going to be able to do too much for you. I can't, understand? I'm employed by the zoo and I'm paid to treat our animals. The fact is, people come here all the time with their wild animals and want me to help them. I tell them the same thing I'm telling you. I can't, as much as I'd like to. But in this case I'll make a slight exception. I'll examine your squirrel and then you can take her to a veterinarian somewhere near you and have him call me and I'll tell him what to do. Okay?"

"That would be wonderful," I said. "There's just one problem."

"What is it?"

"I can't let Chippy out of the box."

"Why not?"

"Because, Doctor," I said sadly, "if I let her out I'll never be able to catch her again."

"You mean she isn't tame?" he asked.

"No, she isn't," I said.

"And you've had her over a year?"

I nodded.

"You mean you can't even hold her?"

I let him see my thumb.

"Oh, sometimes," I said. "But she would never let me do it here, in a strange place, with a stranger in the room."

He gazed at me bewilderedly. "Then how am I supposed to examine her?" he asked. "I can't see anything but her nose in there."

I shrugged helplessly and turned away. I had known that it would come to this.

For a minute Dr. Harrison didn't say anything, and there was silence except for the lions roaring and the peacocks screeching and the typing and voice of the zoo director from Upstate New York coming in faintly from the outer office.

"I'll tell you what," the doctor said at last. "You let her out of the box and I'll catch her as she comes out."

"You won't be able to hold her," I said. "Believe me. She'll tear you all up."

"Go ahead, let her out," he said. "I'll take all the responsibility for anything that happens."

I could see that he had begun to think of the situation as a challenge.

"Don't worry," he said, getting a little excited. "It will be all right."

"Okay," I said.

I started to untie the wire mesh, and the doctor leaned over the desk in front of the box with his hands held as if he was going to catch a ball.

Chippy came out of the box like a Polaris missile out of the ocean. She neatly faked the doctor, leaping right over his hands. She ran up his right arm and down his left and then

back up to his right shoulder. From there she made a spectacular carom off my left shoulder and landed on the top shelf of a long, tall bookcase.

I can't remember very clearly what happened after that, because I know that I tried subconsciously to block the scene from my mind while it was going on. The office was large, so there was plenty of room for Chippy to maneuver in, and in her desperation she performed prodigies of evasion, running over desks and under them and up and down chairs and flinging herself onto bookshelves. Sometimes she would take to the floor, although it had no carpet on it and it was difficult for her to get good traction with her claws on the bare wood. She was so clever at anticipating every move the doctor made that he often found himself looking for her under a chair at one end of the room while she was already under a desk at the other end.

The saddest part of the whole affair was that Chippy kept looking to me to help her escape from the doctor, and every time I came near her she would jump on me and hide from him behind my back whenever he made a lunge for her. She still considered me a friend even though I had brought her to that place, and I knew that she couldn't understand why I always carried her toward the doctor when she jumped on me rather than trying to elude him. I didn't attempt to put a finger on her myself. I knew better. And although the doctor tried very hard to catch her, he couldn't lay a finger on her either.

In the midst of the melee Dr. Green, the director of the zoo, entered the office, which he shared with Dr. Harrison, and promptly joined in on the chase. He really had no choice. Chippy was rapidly destroying the room. But Dr. Green had made the mistake of leaving the door open behind him. Chippy thought she saw a way to freedom and dashed between the legs of the two doctors and through the door and into the outer office. I went after her, just in time to see her race up the leg of the man with the cigar. She ran all over him, and in one of the world's greatest exhibitions of cool he kept right on talking and never even acknowledged Chippy's presence on his person by so much as the batting of an eyelash until she ran out on his right arm toward the hand that held the cigar. Then he swatted at her absently, as if at a bothersome mosquito. She leaped onto the desk, made one of her classic quick puddles right in front of the zoo attendant who was talking to the man with the cigar, and from there she jumped to my shoulder.

I carried her back into the inner office and closed the door, and it all began again. At one point in the middle of it all something poignant happened. Chippy was on top of the long bookcase once more. I stood below her, thinking that she would jump down on my shoulder, as she had already done countless times, never seeming to lose completely her faith in me as a friend. I stood with my elbow raised toward her, which was always my signal that I wanted her to jump, but this time she paused. She was standing at the very end of the bookcase, and a solemn look had come into her eyes. I knew what the look meant, and I waved away the two doctors, who had come up beside me, waiting to try to catch Chippy as soon as she jumped on my shoulder. I said, "No, we can't disturb her now."

Chippy sat up straight, with her toes curled over the end of the bookcase, and she began the elaborate and precise ritual of washing her face and fur and grooming her tail. She closed her eyes tightly and rocked her head back and forth, sneezing moisture onto her stubby thumbs. (Squirrels have almost no saliva in their mouths, so they must get the moisture they need for bathing from their noses.) Then she put her hands in back of her ears and drew them down over her ears and across her eyes and down her nose, time after time. After her face was taken care of, she washed the rest of her fur by rubbing her nose over it directly, sneezing away industriously as she went along. Then she grasped her left forearm in her right hand and drew her left hand up to her teeth and trimmed her nails quickly and expertly. When she had trimmed the nails on her right hand, she grabbed hold of her tail and gave it a thorough comb-out with her teeth, working from the base out to the tip.

I never knew what made Chippy decide that it was time for a bath. She bathed many times a day, and it always began the same way, with her suddenly interrupting whatever she was doing and getting that funny look in her eyes, as if she expected the whole world to stop whatever it was doing too for the ritual. I suppose she had picked up a lot of dust on her fur in all her frantic running around. Anyway, even at a time like that she had to make sure that she was looking her best.

When she was through bathing I held up my elbow again

and she jumped down. The doctors grabbed at her and missed, and they all continued where they had left off, but not me. I no longer wanted any part of it. I simply could not chase that frightened little animal one step further, even if it was for her own good. I sat down on a bench with my back to the room and wouldn't even look at it any more. I was soaked with sweat and my headache was almost unbearable.

I thought the chase would never end, but all of a sudden a door slammed and then there was silence. I looked around and saw that Chippy and Dr. Harrison had vanished. Dr. Green pointed toward the bathroom door, which was closed, and I remembered that it had been standing open before.

"She ran in there," Dr. Green said. "Fred's in there with her. He'll catch her now."

The silence continued, except for an occasional muffled thud from the bathroom that brought to mind those police movies in which you hear muffled thuds from behind a closed door and you know they're in there trying to make somebody sing.

Finally the thuds stopped and the door opened slowly. Dr. Harrison came out holding Chippy in his left hand. He didn't look too good. He had won the war, yes, but he had lost some battles along the way. He was wearing one of those little white doctor's jackets that button up the side and have short sleeves and round collars, and there was a good deal of blood on it. He had gashes from Chippy's back claws along his right forearm, down the right side of his face and across his throat.

I was appalled at the sight of him. I wanted to get down on my knees and beg his forgiveness for what my squirrel had done to him.

"My God, I'm sorry," I said.

He wasn't pleased, but he wasn't angry either.

"It's all right," he said.

I looked down at Chippy. She was lying on her back in his hand, with his thumb held firmly under her chin. She looked subdued and limp. But still there was a look in her eye of the kid who's saying, "Yeah, but you should see the other guy."

"She was doing all right until she started trying to climb up the wall," Dr. Harrison said. "That's when I got her." He looked down at her. "She's not even tensed up now. They always know when they've had it."

He went over and talked to Dr. Green for a minute and then returned to me. "Come on," he said.

He led me through the outer office to a laboratory at the other end of the building. On a table a large animal that looked like some sort of mountain goat was lying on its side, and a woman in a long white coat was giving it an injection.

"Any better?" the doctor asked.

"Much," the woman said. She looked inquiringly at his wounds and at Chippy.

"We had a bit of a roughhouse," the doctor said.

He examined Chippy under a bright light.

"She's got a cyst in there," he said. "Listen, as long as I've gone this far with her, I'm going to go ahead and fix her up."

Still holding Chippy in his left hand, he operated on her with his right, and I was very proud of her because although he used no anesthetic she never flinched or struggled once during the procedure. When it was over, the doctor said that he thought she would be all right now. I asked him how I could repay him, but he just said not to worry about it.

He gazed at Chippy thoughtfully. "The problem is, how

are we going to get her back in her box so you can take her home?"

I got a cold feeling in the pit of my stomach. I could envision him letting her go and the chase starting all over again.

"I have a little theory," he said. "I think that if I set her on your shoulder and you go back to my office and put her down close to her box, she'll run right inside it."

Without giving me time to think twice about it, he put Chippy on my shoulder. I walked back to his office with my heart beating wildly and leaned down beside the desk, and just as the doctor had said she would, Chippy ran into her box. At that, we tied the wire mesh back over the front of the box, and for the first time in hours I breathed freely.

I thanked Dr. Harrison and Dr. Green, and then I hurried out to my car and headed home.

When I got back to my house I immediately set to work to restore order in Chippy's cage. With her still in her house, I tied the house back on its branch, and then I put the screen back over the top of the cage and the beach towels on top of the screen. Then I opened the door of the cage and took the wire mesh off the front of her house. Chippy came out and jumped onto my shoulder and from there leaped up to the top of her cage. She rolled around on the beach towels for a while. Then I got her a piece of fresh cold peach from the refrigerator. She ate it hungrily and then rolled around some more. The swelling was all gone, and she was a happy squirrel again.

Eight RIGHT AFTER the beginning of the new year
(1967), my sister and her husband decided to go on a two-
week vacation to Hawaii. They asked me if I would stay
in their house, which was about fifteen miles from where I
lived, while they were gone and look after their teen-aged
daughter, who, of course, was in school and couldn't make
the trip with them.

I said I would, and then immediately I started trying to
figure out what to do about Chippy. Obviously I would
have to take her with me, but the memory of my expedition
with her to the zoo was still fresh, and the very thought of
moving her from one place to another for any reason what-
soever was painful. I had about two weeks to think it over,
and finally I realized that inevitably I was going to have to
go through the horror of trapping Chippy in her house
again. The plan I had come up with involved transporting
her cage in my brother-in-law's station wagon, and I didn't
think it would be a good idea to leave the squirrel in her cage
while it was lying on its side in the back of the station
wagon.

Very simply, my strategy was to trap Chippy in her house, as before, remove the house from the cage, as before, stick the cage in the back of the car, put the squirrel in her house on the front seat beside me, as before, and drive to my destination as fast as possible.

The fateful day came. I drove the vacationers to the airport in the station wagon and then went home. I put on my pigskin gloves and scared Chippy into her house and tied the piece of wire mesh that I had used the last time over the entrance to the box once again. I removed the house from the cage and put it on the living-room table. Then I started to take the cage down and load it into the station wagon, but I never even made it out the door, because Chippy, who must have done some heavy brooding about her last experience of being trapped in her house, was not having any of it this time.

Instead of gnawing futilely on the wire mesh as she had done before, she had set right to work on the side of her house, which was made of wood half an inch thick. There were three small round windows on each side of the house, and Chippy started gnawing on one of the middle windows and never stopped until she had enlarged it to the point where it was big enough for her to pop out of. It was an amazing thing to watch. First, there was just the tip of her nose sticking out, and then pretty soon there was the whole squirrel coming through. The gnawing was accompanied by some fairly pathetic squealing, but that was just dramatics, and the entire break-out, from start to finish, didn't take more than ten minutes.

I knew when I was beaten. I put the house back in the cage, and Chippy stayed home while I lived at my sister's house. I visited her every morning for a couple of hours, to fix up her cage and replenish her food supply and let her out of the cage and play with her, and she didn't seem to mind the arrangement at all.

It was during one of my morning visits to Chippy that my phone rang and I was given some shocking news. It seemed that the person from whom I rented the house had just signed a contract with 20th Century–Fox permitting them to use the property as the principal location for a Frank Sinatra film called *Tony Rome* that was to begin shooting in April.

I was stunned, but there was nothing I could do. I had no lease but just a vague unwritten agreement, and it was an opportunity for the owner to make some extra income from the property.

After the phone call I stood looking out the windows in the living room at the sunken garden and the silent wilderness all around, and I tried to imagine the place full of sound trucks and cameras, generators, klieg lights and movie people. What would the raccoons and the spotted-breasted orioles and the squirrels make of it? What would the foxes think? To say nothing of Chippy. It was impossible for me to believe that after so long my world away from the world was about to become unsecret, unprivate, known, occupied, explored, scrutinized, perhaps even famous.

The next morning, when I arrived for my visit with Chippy, there were Cadillacs in the driveway, and men were prowling all over the place, measuring vistas, framing shots with their fingers and taking Polaroid pictures of everything, and I knew that I had better believe it.

*Chippy was a
bottle-fed baby.*

*No place like home. Chippy peers out of the picture window in her
bedroom, high on the branch in the top part of her cage.*

A routine inspection of territory . . .

a jump to . . .

found treasure from under the bed and
a moment's rest on a bureau.

bookshelves . . .

chair . . . and shoulder;

Lunchtime.

A spider plant is always a reliable hiding place for nuts . . .

"I know I hid more in here somewhere."

*How to brush
a squirrel.*

*Chippy at the doughnut window with her favorite birthday present,
a pink hibiscus. Just after the picture was taken, she ate it, naturally.*

The cave in the sunken garden where the baby foxes were born. All the vines that covered it have been removed, revealing a strange little replica of an Indian village at the cave's entrance.

Seen from the sunken garden, the stairs that the author climbed to give water to the ocelot, chased up to the landing by the foxes.

Truly històric ground. The stretch of the driveway where the author met the father fox on his fateful return to the property, and where he saw Chippy come back after her first and second adventures in the trees. At left center—the gnarled sapodilla tree, its trunk worn smooth by generations of squirrels. At right center, the curved base of Mother Squirrel's palm, from which Chippy may have fallen when she landed in the clutches of Bella, the cat.

91

A view of the royal palms, roughly 80 feet tall, in the front field. Chippy climbed the center tree, with its curved, sunlit trunk, to take her long nap.

Gay Fairbairn and Spooky.

Douglas Fairbairn and Billy Blue Jay.

Part Two

Nine

FINALLY A morning came when I went outside quite early and saw a group of men all squatting in a circle in the driveway over on the other side of the swimming pool, and I knew instinctively that whatever was going to happen was about to happen now. I had known that somebody was out there because Chippy had interrupted her rounds to stare out her window and flick her tail periodically while I had been having my coffee, and I had heard voices and car doors slamming. But I hadn't bothered to pull back the curtains and look out myself. Lately, I had begun to think that the less I knew about what was happening the better. Then, a little later, I passed by the men on my way to my car, and I could see clearly that they were not of the same breed as the ones who had come before. They weren't going to stroll around in the sunshine smoking cigars and taking pictures and chatting pleasantly among themselves for a little while and then get back into their cars and go away. These men had a set of blueprints laid out on the ground that they were studying intently, and they were dressed in work clothes and looked dismayingly like the men who were tearing down the old houses and putting up the new buildings all around me.

There were about a dozen of them. They looked up at me curiously as I went past, and I nodded to them and they nodded to me. I went on down the driveway and paused at the shocking sight that greeted me. Each of the men had brought his own car. These cars were parked helter-skelter all over the back lot, and since they were the kind of cars that the American workman traditionally uses for going to the job in, cars that on used-car lots are always referred to as "transportation specials," the place had suddenly been transformed from a woodland glade into a junkyard. I was seeing cars where I had never seen cars before—cars on the grass, cars jammed in between the trees, cars with their bumpers pushed into the cacti and the frangipani. I saw that a section of bark had been scraped off an ironwood tree, and already crumpled cigarette packages and chewing-gum wrappers lay on the grass and butts had been ground out on the driveway.

I drove down to the village and came back about an hour later. By this time a large truck had arrived and was parked squarely in the middle of the driveway so that I couldn't go to my usual parking place, which was in the shade of a sapodilla tree, but had to park out in the open on the grass among the cars belonging to the workmen. The rear of the truck was open, and a man inside was passing out lumber to the workmen. As I went along the driveway toward the house I heard shouting and hammering, and as I came around the bend at the ficus tree I saw that the men were laying out a boundary with stakes and boards on the wide expanse of lawn between the house and the swimming pool. A boundary for what? I wondered, going past them. We all nodded again.

I went upstairs and tried to do some writing, but I couldn't concentrate. I had to keep getting up and going to the window to see what was going on outside. Once when I went to the window I saw that three of the workmen were standing below my windows staring up at Chippy as she sailed excitedly around in her cage. When they saw me they turned away and went back to their hammering. A little later I saw several of them wandering around in the sunken garden, looking into the cave and the pump house. And then still later I saw some of them coming out of the trees on the far side of the swimming pool, and I knew that they had discovered the dark pond and the shaft leading down to the tunnel.

As the day wore on the level of the noise and the amount of general milling around outside increased steadily. An electric saw with a particularly earsplitting and morale-shattering whine was introduced. The truck kept lumbering away and rumbling back again with more lumber. And I noticed that the men had begun staking out a second boundary in the back lot.

Naturally I had tried to get the owner of the property to give me some idea of what it was going to be like when work on the picture began, but the answers had been vague. First, they were going to build some sets. That would take about a month. Then the shooting would begin. That would take only four or five days. Then they were going to dismantle the sets, collect all their debris and go away, leaving the place exactly as they had found it. Also, I was assured, the "movie people" had been told that I was a writer and they had sworn to make every effort to see that I was not disturbed or inconvenienced. In other words, according to the owner, I was to carry on as usual and just to ignore the movie people altogether. That had sounded fishy at the time, and it sounded even fishier now. How could I ignore the "movie people"? It would have been like trying to ignore a bombardment. And what efforts were they making to keep from disturbing me? I had already been disturbed all I wanted to be, and this was only the first day. Then the business about leaving the place exactly as they had found it. How was that going to be possible when they had already begun smashing into trees and knocking down shrubs and driving all over the grass?

I found myself pacing the floor restlessly. I wanted to go outside and prowl around the place as I usually did several times a day. But I didn't want to be stared at, watched, observed or even wondered about.

I kept on pacing, and then gradually I began to take a different view. To hell with it, I thought. Why should I be so self-conscious? What did I care about the "movie people" and what they thought of me?

I went out on the terrace and cleaned the birdbath and filled it with fresh water. Then I crumbled a doughnut on the window ledge. However, the birds didn't come right away, and I didn't see any squirrels around either. I also noticed that the tabby cats, as was their custom whenever things began to look threatening, had voted with their feet and disappeared. I ambled around, trying to look blasé, as if it meant nothing to me that the place was swarming with strangers, and finally I went around the swimming pool and down the hill, hoping to see the foxes. Of course there was no sign of them, and I imagined that they were back in the darkest part of the woods, listening to all the racket that the workmen were making and trying to figure out what it portended.

Down in the front part of the property it was peaceful. I

could hear the hammering and the shouting and the whine of the saw only faintly, and I felt at home again. I sat on the curving trunk of a coconut palm that had fallen in a hurricane long ago and looked across the sunny field at the female sparrow hawk perched on the telephone wire that ran above the hedge that separated my property from the field next to it. The little hawk came every winter and perched on exactly the same spot on the wire all day in good weather. On stormy days I never saw her. From the wire she hunted insects and lizards, swooping down on them suddenly with a shrill cry that I always thought must have stopped their hearts before she ever hit them. The wire was not her preferred observation post. She would much rather have perched on the highest branch of a flowering tree that rose halfway up the hill. From there she had a panoramic view not only of my field but of the ones on either side of it and the road and the field across the road. Occasionally she would perch up there and I would see her, proud, alert, just a white speck against the sky, quivering slightly in the wind, high above everything. But she could never get away with it for very long, because soon enough the blue jays and the cardinals and the orioles would discover her and fly up and start screaming at her and pestering her by diving back and forth at her. No matter how hard she tried to resist them with sheer stoicism and severe looks, they always won in the end, and she had to go back down to the wire.

It was difficult to follow the birds' reasoning. If it was all right for the sparrow hawk to perch on the wire, why wasn't it all right for her to perch on the tree? They never bothered her when she was on the wire, and yet that section of the wire was just as much in their territory as the tree. But the sparrow hawk was really just as bad as they were.

She wouldn't allow the marsh hawk that lurked in the tall pines on the slope to come down and perch on the limb of a scraggly little pine that he was very fond of at the edge of the field. When he did come down the sparrow hawk got hysterical and flew in circles around him, crying shrilly and endlessly. The marsh hawk always seemed to think that she would wear herself out eventually and leave him alone, so he, as they say, hung in there. As a result, the sparrow hawk would have to spend whole afternoons fussing at him, and when she became particularly desperate she would go racing around far and wide, as if she wanted to tell the entire neighborhood about the unbelievable nerve of the marsh hawk who was trying to invade her territory. She always triumphed finally, and the marsh hawk would go back to the high pines, where he would be quite invisible except for the times when he caught a young bird. Then the blue jays and the cardinals and the orioles would surround him and scold him furiously, and, knowing where he was then, I would go out with my field glasses and look at him. Even with the dead bird in his talons he always seemed to be trying to look perfectly innocent, as if he couldn't for the life of him understand how anyone would suspect him of foul play.

I looked for the foxes again, didn't see them, and went back up to the house and spent the rest of the morning and afternoon working and waiting for it to be quitting time for the workmen so that they would leave and I would be alone again. When they finally went away, around five o'clock, I went outside and looked over the scene they had left behind them. They seemed to have made good progress with whatever it was that they were building, and they had strewn the ground with bent nails, pop bottles, gum wrappers, broken pencils, matchbooks and cigarette butts.

I was surprised to find that I was not quite alone. A man in an impressive powder-blue, dove-gray and gold uniform with a big pistol in a black holster hanging from his belt stood in the entrance to the swimming pool. I jumped slightly at the sight of him, and then I remembered the owner telling me that the movie people would insist on having a guard on the premises all night to guard their equipment and the sets.

The guard said hello, and I said hello to him. He was middle-aged, overweight and already looked bored to death.

"Are you the guy who lives here?" he asked, taking a small notebook out of his breast pocket.

I said I was.

"Okay," he said, making a note. "You don't own the place, do you?"

"No, I just rent it," I said.

He looked around. "Man, if this ain't creepsville," he said. "What kind of a movie are they going to make here anyway? Some kind of a creep movie?"

"I don't know what kind of a movie it's going to be," I said.

"It's gotta be vampires," he said. "Listen, what happens around here at night?"

"What do you mean?" I asked.

"Well, don't tell me that half the snakes and scorpions in Dade County don't start coming out from under the rocks right after it gets dark around here. I was bitten by a scorpion once, you know, and I can still feel it in my big toe every time it rains. In fact, I'm lucky I didn't die, that's how bad it was. So don't tell me about scorpions, okay? Listen, you actually *pay* to live here?"

"I sure do," I said.

"Well, I've got news for you," he said, hitching up his gun belt. "I wouldn't live here if *you* paid *me*. I'm not kidding. This place is decrepit. How long has it been since this swimming pool was filled, for instance?"

"Quite a while," I said.

"I believe you. You know what this place reminds me of? Did you ever see that movie *Sunset Boulevard?* Bill Holden and Gloria Swanson? Creepy, overgrown place like this out in Hollywood? Hey, maybe this is a remake of *Sunset Boulevard*. That's not such a bad idea. Who's going to be in it anyway?"

"Frank Sinatra."

"Yeah?"

The guard was impressed. He whistled softly and made a face, pulling down the corners of his mouth and rolling his eyes up toward the ficus tree.

"Well, now you're showing me a little class," he said.

He sat down on one of the benches beside the swimming pool, leaned back, crossed his legs and lit a cigarette.

"What a fantastic waste," he said, looking around at the property again. "You know what I'd do if I owned this place? First of all, I'd bring in a bulldozer and knock down that godforsaken old house and remove all this *growth*. Then I'd slap in a high-rise so fast it would make your head swim. And I wouldn't just sell the place outright to some builder either. I'd want a piece of the action. I'd want a down payment of maybe . . . What's this land worth anyway if you had it all cleaned up and ready to go? Quarter of a mill? Half a mill? Well, I'd take a down payment of a quarter of a mill anyway, and then I'd take a percentage of the gross, plus which I'd want my own apartment rent-free for life up on the top floor. And then I'd just sit up there and watch the checks roll in, and I don't want to know nothing."

When it was almost dark I took a package of chicken necks to the foxes. The guard was sitting on the swimming-pool balustrade eating a sandwich and drinking coffee from a Thermos when I went past him. I knew that he saw the chicken necks and I also supposed that he heard me when I stood near the pond and clucked for the foxes, but at that point I was beyond caring.

Later on, when I went out, I saw that the guard had pulled his car up next to the swimming pool and was sitting inside with the door open, listening to a transistor radio. When I returned a few hours later he was sleeping soundly on the front seat, perhaps dreaming of the checks rolling in.

Ten   As THE days went by and the movie people multiplied and their sets grew larger and the noise they made increased, one of the results of their intrusion into my life was that I was forced to do something that nobody really likes to do unless he happens to be a flaming success, which I certainly wasn't. I was forced to take a good long hard look at myself, to try to see myself as I really was or as others saw me, and it wasn't a very pretty sight. Who likes to admit, for one thing, that he's living an oddball existence if he's past twenty-five or so? No one, unless he's crazy, and then it's a whole different thing anyway.

What I'm saying is that there I was, living in a spooky old house with a squirrel, communicating with a bunch of foxes and some birds, never having any visitors, working on a novel to which there seemed to be no end and not getting one second younger.

Every once in a while one of the workmen would say to me, "Say, what's that you've got in your house—a squirrel?"

They knew. They didn't have to mess around.

"That's right," I would say.

"No kidding? How long have you had him?"

"Her," I would say.

"Huh?"

"Had *her*. She's a female."

"Oh. So how long have you had her?"

"Going on two years."

"No kidding? Well, aren't you going to let her go?"

"I tried to let her go once," I would say. "But she came back."

"Yeah? That's cute."

Then they would give me the look. I knew what they were thinking. "You meatball."

To them I was the guy with the squirrel or, more properly, "the guy who lives here who's supposed to be a writer and—are you sitting down?—has a squirrel living in the house with him." The fact is, there just isn't much dignity in being either a person who is "supposed to be a writer" or a squirrel owner—and to be both! Simultaneously! If I had been "the guy who lives here who's supposed to be a writer and has a *lion* living in the house with him," it would have been different. Or a *bear*, or a *tiger*, or a *water buffalo*. Then I would still have been a meatball, but at least an interesting sort of meatball, because lions, bears, tigers and water buffalo are impressive. Squirrels, on the other hand, are not impressive. Not on the level of size and destructive potential anyway, which is what most people admire in a wild animal.

Even my friends had their doubts about me (you always know when your friends have their doubts about you). I'm sure that they thought my having a squirrel was a symptom of something but they just didn't know quite what. (I was forty years old. All kinds of things can begin happening to

you when you turn forty, usually none of them any good.)
They had been willing to go along with it in the beginning.
They had even encouraged me when I had first brought
Chippy into my home to keep her and take care of her, and
they had had many hearty chuckles over my stories about
her when she was young. But by now, Chippy had become
to them just a part of my own strange existence, and I could
tell they were concerned about it.

As for my reputation as a writer, I simply didn't have one.
Which was rather a hard pill to swallow when I was, at that
time, the author of five published novels. It was just that
nobody had ever read any of them, or even heard of them,
much less of me. And that was why I was still, at my age,
someone who was "supposed to be a writer," meaning someone who—it is known, one way or another—has been published but whose work is totally unfamiliar to everyone
except his agent and his desperately unhappy publisher. I
would say that in the scale of indifference that the average
man feels for writers in general, the writer who is "supposed
to be a writer" ranks far below even the "would-be writer."
At least the "would-be writer" may have possibilities, but
the writer who is "supposed to be a writer" has obviously
had his chance and has failed. Otherwise, why doesn't he
have a Continental? Why does he have that funny look in
his eyes? And when you ask him the names of his books,
why do they all sound strained or slightly phony, or as if
they had been taken either from something by Shakespeare
or "Dover Beach"?

The novel I was working on was called *Collie Welles*. It
had started out as a short story, which I had thought would
run to about twenty pages. Three years later the story had
become a novel, and it had now gone over five hundred

pages. The writing went slowly and painfully. There was much rewriting. The end kept receding, and there were times when I thought I never would finish. I couldn't work on anything else because the book obsessed me, but it was breaking me. I was spending every dime I had on it, and the prospects were that eventually I would have to go far into debt for it. The worst part was that no one was encouraging me to continue with the book. Usually a writer can count on his editor to cheer him on when the burden of his work has become more than he can bear alone, but my editor at the publishing house that had published my last novel, in 1964, had been dead against this book from the beginning—because it was completely unlike anything I had written before. (At the same time my agent was telling me that the reason I had never gotten anywhere with my writing was that I had never taken any chances.) When I had sent him the first fifty pages he had advised me to abandon the book immediately. When I had persisted anyway and had sent him the first two hundred pages later on, he had told me to abandon the book again, and we had exchanged some bitter words over the manuscript—he hating it and I defending it—and we had finally broke off our relationship forever, both on the personal level and on the official level, with the result that I had suddenly found myself in the precarious position of being in the middle of a long novel with no publisher and no contract, a condition that would give almost any writer deep feelings of anxiety.

Then, the place where I lived. There was no question but that I had become too attached to it and too possessive of it, and the unreasonableness of my attachment and my possessiveness was revealed in my hostility toward the movie people. I resented them. Perhaps I even hated them. They were spoiling the place. They were exposing it. They were ridiculing it. They despised it. They wanted to use it as a location not because they thought it was beautiful but because they thought it was, as the guard had said, creepy. (Although none of the movie crew seemed to have a clear idea of what the movie they were working on was about, I had found out that the main set they were building was going to be the façade of an old mansion that was supposed to have been empty for the past nineteen years. It was going to be covered with palm fronds and vines and generally made to look as if it had been through two or three major hurricanes—and to this house Frank Sinatra was to come, looking for a man who was lurking there, who had something to do with a murder that he, Frank Sinatra, playing a detective named Tony Rome, was investigating.)

I knew that I shouldn't have let any of it bother me. After all, I didn't *own* the place. What was it to me, really? Why care so much about it? My concern would have been appropriate if it had been Walden and I had been Henry David Thoreau. But it wasn't Walden and I wasn't Henry David Thoreau. I was just a tenant living in an old house on an overgrown piece of land that was only about two jumps ahead of the developers. It was crazy of me to care so much about those three acres. To care so much about them put me out of step with the way of thinking of practically everybody in that entire section of the country, and particularly with my own community, which was largely made up of airline personnel, junior-college students and kids who had run away from home. Everybody was from Philadelphia, Chicago or Los Angeles, and nobody intended to stay around long. It was crazy of me to walk around the place and suddenly stop, as I often did, looking at the trees and thinking, Pretty soon none of this will be here, as if that would be the end of the world. It wouldn't be the end of the world. I would go on. I would move, many times. I was as much an American as anybody else, and we were a nation of nomads, right? I would forget all about the sunken gardens, the foxes, the spotted-breasted orioles. I would have other problems. I would change. And if I had owned the land myself there would have been nothing I could have done to prevent its ultimate destruction anyway. Very rich people were selling off their houses on the ridge all the time and moving into condominiums, because the taxes, which were already confiscatory, were going up constantly, and pressure for rezoning was ferocious and getting more ferocious every day.

What I'm saying is that not long after the movie people came I began waking up around five o'clock every morning, and lying there in the darkness and the silence, waiting for dawn, all I could think about was what I had begun to conceive as the truth about myself—which was, in essence, that for a long time now I had been trying to avoid facing up to the fact that I was a failure as a writer, that my present way of life was actually nothing more than part of my attempt to escape this reality and that no matter how hard I might work at my writing and for how long, I would still remain a failure. My whole existence was a syndrome of failure—the creepy place where I lived, my difficult pet, my impossible novel. It was all so terribly clear to me at five o'clock in the morning.

Soon, lying there, I would hear Chippy rattling around in her house out in the living room as she awakened. Then I would hear her go down to the bottom of her cage and snuffle around in her newspaper, looking for a couple of sunflower seeds or a piece of lettuce to put her on her feet. And finally she would begin her rounds. Before, all of those little morning sounds from my squirrel had been reassuring. They had signaled the start of a new day full of new chances. Now they were depressing. They just meant the beginning of another leg on the long journey to oblivion.

When I finally dragged myself out of bed, still tired from not having slept too well, aching from having tossed and turned so long before having been able to drop off to sleep at all, and went to the living room to sit by the window and have my first precious cup of coffee of the day, it wasn't the same as it had been. Before, that had been a pleasant, even magic moment, sitting there, gazing at the sunken garden and the lawn and the trees, aware of Chippy on her rounds and of the cardinals and orioles fluttering in the sapodilla tree wanting to attract my attention so that I would come out with some doughnuts for them. Now Chippy made me nervous, and what I saw out the window was piles of lumber, miscellaneous junk and the backside of a monstrous movie set. Then the car doors would start slamming out in the back lot, and the workmen would come shambling along the driveway. The truck would arrive. The hammering and the shouting and the whine of the saw would begin.

Before, I had been happy—perhaps the happiest I had ever been in my life, although I guess I hadn't thought of it exactly that way. I had just accepted it and lived it. Everything about my simple, limited life had seemed to make reasonably good sense and to be pretty good fun.

Now I was not happy. I wanted to get out of there. That was what I kept saying to myself. "I've got to get out of here." I didn't want any more of any of it. No more foxes, no more birds, no more cutting grass, raking, hauling palm fronds to the road. I neglected Chippy. I didn't feel like playing with her any more. I stopped working on my novel altogether. I couldn't even bear to think about it. What I felt like doing was taking Chippy out and sticking her in an oak tree, putting everything I owned in storage, telling my friends and relations goodbye and taking off. My only problem was that I didn't know where I would go or what I would do when I got there. In the back of my mind I suppose what I really wanted to do was to go down to the docks and get a job on a yacht. Sailing on yachts was about the only sort of job that I had ever worked at for any length of time that I had liked much, and when I thought about being out there on the ocean with the salt spray in my face, free of problems, free of ambition, free of any worries because everything is taken care of and thought out for you on the yachts, as in the Army, it seemed like a wonderful idea. But something held me and kept me from running away to sea. Instead I just took to sitting around all day, staring at the walls.

Eleven   It was April. Ordinarily the rains began in late April, but this year the weather continued beautiful day after day, not only clear but also quite cool. I kept thinking that one of these days the deluge would begin, and then what? The movie people didn't seem to know anything about the spring rains in Florida, which are rather like the monsoon. They were just bop-bop-bopping along as if they had never heard of such a thing. On the one hand I thought that if the rains began soon enough they might get discouraged and decide to pack up and go and make the thing in Los Angeles, but on the other hand I was afraid they wouldn't do anything of the kind but would just delay the whole production for a couple of months and that would mean I would have them out there all through the summer.

So I spent part of the time hoping for the rains to come and part of the time hoping they wouldn't, and meanwhile the building of the sets progressed. The main set, by the swimming pool, soon began to look convincingly like what it was supposed to be—an old house that hadn't been lived in for a long time. It was a two-story house, pink with white trim and with a red tile roof. On one end there was a terrace with a balustrade around it copied after the balustrade around the swimming pool, a screened-in porch, old-fashioned windows with little panes and ledges, and at the other end there was a tall square tower, rather fortresslike and spooky-looking with only a few windows set deep in what were made to look like very thick walls.

Across from the house, on the other side of the swimming pool, in a clearing near the foxes' pond, was a deep hole in the ground. At first the men had tried to dig the hole themselves with picks and shovels, but the hard white coral rock had defeated them. Then they had called in a gigantic red machine that had huffed and puffed and shuddered as its great claw had pounded the rock and broken it up finally and scooped it out of the ground. No one seemed to know what the hole was for, but it was about six feet long and three feet wide and six feet deep, and it looked like a grave.

Out in the back lot a separate group of men was building another house, but this one was much smaller. And down in front, in the middle of the field that the sparrow hawk watched over, there was a pile of lumber waiting to be made, someone told me, into a potting shed.

In the evenings, after the workmen had left, I would often sit on a concrete seat that stood at the edge of the clearing across the swimming pool from the main set. The seat had a high back and Sphinx faces on the arms and obscure figures in bas relief across the back, and it was overhung by clouds of hibiscus and oleander. In fact it was almost enveloped by hibiscus and oleander. Anyway it was terribly uncomfortable. But it was remote and a good place from which to gaze across the open grave and the swimming pool at the last of the sun blazing on the façade of the make-believe house. In that light and with the workmen gone the house looked astonishingly solid and permanent. The strange thing was that the more solid and permanent the house looked the more alienated I felt from the piece of property on which it stood. I found myself simply not being able to care about a lot of things that I had cared so much about before, and it was a sad feeling.

There were two guards now, one for the front gate and one for the back. They argued passionately but in low voices about dog racing and pro football, either sitting by the pool or strolling back and forth along the driveway. With increasing frequency they had to chase out interlopers. The word was getting around in the village that a movie was in production, and a lot of people wanted to come and see the sets and perhaps catch a glimpse of Frank Sinatra.

Sometimes in the evening I went to the pond and called the foxes and walked all over looking for them, but I didn't see them any more. I never even saw them in my headlights late at night, so I knew they were gone. But most of the other animals around the place had adjusted themselves to the presence of the movie people. The cats, for instance, after their initial defection had returned in force and were carrying on with their lives just as before. In the midst of all the confusion and noise during the day they went right on with their fighting and their intensely complicated love affairs, but at high noon they would all declare a truce and gather in the shade on the driveway at a point where a soft breeze wafted up the hill from the bay. The workmen had to step over and around them as they went about their business. Now and then the ghastly screech of a cat with a stepped-on tail would freeze the air, but in general the workmen had adjusted to the cats just as the cats had adjusted to the workmen.

The squirrels had come back to the doughnut window along with the birds, and the birds splashed in the bath on the terrace just as joyously as always. A mockingbird that had built her nest on a low branch of a large seagrape that reached out quite near a corner of the main set soon had a nestful of babies. I had happened to see the nest one day when I was walking around, and I had been afraid that when the eggs hatched the babies would start peeping all the time and attract the attention of the workmen and then there would be trouble. But the babies never let out a sound, and I don't think the workmen were ever aware of the nest, even though some of them ate their lunches every day sitting on the grass right below it. And, remarkably, the mother mockingbird never got mean and flew at them, which is something they always do when they feel that their babies are endangered. Mockingbirds are relentless and fierce cat-and-dog chasers, and it was not an uncommon sight in the nesting season to see one of the cats hustling across the field with its tail down and its belly rubbing the ground as a mockingbird pursued it, nipping at its ears.

Even Chippy got used to the movie people eventually. As long as they didn't create too much of a disturbance she either observed them thoughtfully from her window or else ignored them altogether. What she couldn't get used to was me. She was sensitive to my moods, and she knew that I had suddenly become very unhappy. She saw that the whole routine of my life had changed. She watched me sitting for long periods of time just looking into space. Perhaps she was sympathetic, but anyway she couldn't stand it when I paced the floor, which I had a tendency to do when I was upset. She might be sound asleep in her house, but the minute I

started pacing from room to room she would pop out and fix me with a stern look, and if I kept it up too long she would begin clicking her teeth at me, a warning sound. Worst of all, from her point of view, our games weren't much fun any more. She wanted to play so badly when I let her out of her cage each day that she could barely contain herself, but all I wanted to do was mope. She would run all over me ecstatically, hoping that I would snap out of it. When I didn't respond she started doing everything she could think of that was forbidden, just to make me pay some attention to her. She would disappear into closets and pull things down, climb on the bookcase and knock books over, get into all my papers, chew up my pencils, steal my chessmen and dig in the flower pots. But it didn't work. All I did was continue to mope and keep thinking that I had to get out of there.

Twelve   ONCE THE main set was finished, the atmosphere changed, the tempo picked up, the confusion and the noise got worse and all of the movie people began to act very purposeful. The big men who had come in the Cadillacs in the beginning but had not been seen much of since then began showing up all the time. They would come in big groups and break up into small groups and wander all over the property and then come together again and break up again. There were always conferences going on. Girls with clipboards followed the big men around and made notes of what they said. Couriers arrived and were sent away again. People were summoned from one end of the property to the other and came running and sweating. There were occasional temper tantrums, but that really was to be expected—the first day of shooting was drawing near. On the last day of April I was told that starting on May 4 it was going to be lights, camera, action.

"What fantastic weather!" the movie people kept saying.

I just looked at them. It was fantastic all right. Where was the monsoon? The weather was so good that the movie people were already talking about coming back to Florida the next year to do a sequel.

"Look at that sky!" they would say.

Day after day the sky was the purest blue, and the bright sun shone steadily enough to give any cameraman fits of ecstasy. The air was warm in the middle of the day, but it wasn't absolutely awash with humidity the way it usually was at that time of year. Ideal weather for making movies, in other words, and all of this enthusiasm of the *Tony Rome* company for the south Florida weather led to the reopening of the question of Florida's natural right to become a center of movie-making. Ever since the 1920s chamber-of-commerce boosters had been trying to attract big-time producers to Florida, never with much success. In fact, George Bourke, writing in the Miami *Herald*, said that when an executive from Twentieth Century–Fox came to Miami in the Forties to find out what equipment would be available locally when they began work on a picture called *Slattery's Hurricane* that they intended to make there, he found out that the entire Florida "film industry" at that time possessed only one BNC Mitchel camera, the standard for major studio work, and that there were no camera-servicing, production or laboratory facilities at all.

What nobody knew then was that the unusually dry spring of 1967 was the prelude to a long series of dry springs and falls that was to lead eventually into the tragic drought of 1970 that very nearly destroyed the Everglades.

As it was, dust sometimes obscured the perfect sky, when the wind shifted to the west. The thing that I had known would happen had happened. The enormous number of cars and trucks running over the dry grass out in the back lot had obliterated the grass and turned the whole area into a dust bowl. The dust rose up in tan clouds and hung in the air all day or advanced like fog along the driveway and through the trees. But no one paid any attention to that. They didn't mind dust, and they didn't care about the grass, and things were just starting to get exciting. Heavy trucks carrying lighting equipment had arrived from the Fox studio in California. The trucks were painted dark green and had the Fox emblem painted on the doors. They looked a thousand years old, and you couldn't help wondering how they could have made it all the way across the country.

A specialist from Los Angeles had arrived at about the same time as the lighting trucks. His job was to "age" the main set. He was an important man, an artist really, and everyone treated him with much respect.

Truckloads of shrubbery from nurseries kept coming in, which surely was bringing coals to Newcastle, and the nurserymen dug holes in the ground around the sets and planted the shrubbery in great profusion. The lighting men unloaded the trucks that had come from the Coast and began setting up the lights and laying out the thick black cables that would connect the lights with the central power source for the whole operation, a generator in a huge General Camera trailer truck that was parked on the road just outside the back gate. The lighting men barged through the woods hauling their cables and howling and cursing at "this damn jungle." The jungle was apprehensive. Birds and squirrels fear snakes. The cables must have looked like gigantic black snakes to them. They were silent, watching.

One of the big shots knocked on my door. He had a look of desperation. They had a serious problem, he said, and he wondered if I would help them try to solve it. The problem was the cats. They were afraid that when the shooting began the cats would wander in and out of the shots and start fighting or something and spoil everything. Were they my cats?

"No," I said.

"Whose cats are they?"

"I've never known," I said. "Some of them have homes in the neighborhood, I suppose, but they never seem to spend much time there. Most of them are just strays, I think. To tell you the truth, I've never really tried to keep track of them. They come and go, come and go."

"Well, who feeds them? They look fat enough. You?"

"Very rarely," I said. "They live off the land. They're good that way."

"Well, we've got to do something with them," he said. "We have a tight schedule, you know. We can't be chasing cats around all the time."

Later, I went outside and saw a group of carpenters hard at work near the bottom of my steps. They looked disgruntled and also a little sheepish.

"Say, what's that you're making?" I asked them.

I knew. Anyone could have told at a glance. But these were the same people who had had a good many laughs at my expense, and I wanted to get some of my own back. They looked even more disgruntled.

"Cages," one of them said sourly, not looking up.

"Pardon?" I said.

"Cages!"

"That's what I thought you said. Cages?"

"Cages for the goddam cats!"

Very handsome cages they were too, as they should have been, with such highly paid craftsmen building them. Four roomy cages, made of wood and chicken wire, each with a little door with hinges and a latch. The carpenters considered it infra dig to devote their talents to such a meatball project, and I had a strong feeling that there would be bitter words said about it at the union hall. But they sweated sullenly over the assignment for the rest of the afternoon, and finally, when they were all finished, there was a conference of big shots concerning the cat-cage situation. From my window I could look down and see the big shots gathered around the cages, gazing at them thoughtfully, while in the driveway, unsuspecting, the cats snoozed. I saw the big shots look from the cats to the cages and then back at the cats again. Then they would walk around the cages, sometimes bending over to peer into them, sometimes reaching out tentatively to touch the chicken wire, sometimes testing the doors to see that they worked properly. Then the big shot who had knocked on my door in the first place went over and said something to a minor shot who was in charge of the workmen who had no specific trades but were employed just to look alive and make themselves useful around the location. These men spent a lot of time smoking and lounging about and complaining about working conditions. Now a couple of them who had been lounging in the background observing the big shots were summoned, and I could tell from the look on their faces that what their boss said to them wasn't received enthusiastically. For a moment they stood looking at the cats, and then one of them got down in the traditional here-kitty-kitty position and started saying, "Here, kitty, kitty."

The cats weren't used to that sort of thing. They were used to being yelled at and stepped on. They lifted their heads and stared at the man suspiciously. He glanced back at the big shots, but they just urged him on, so he called to the cats again, extending his thumb and forefinger toward them enticingly, as if he had a gizzard for them. But those cats had not been born yesterday or at any other time in the recent past, and two or three of them got up and stretched and then began slinking away. At that the big shots told the workmen to cut out the subtleties and go and round up the cats and stick them in the cages.

Building nice cages for cats is one thing, but catching the cats and putting them in the cages is quite another. Therefore, a strange spectacle began to unfold below my windows. First it was just the extra workmen chasing the cats and the cats eluding them. Then lighting men and other technicians were called in to help with the chase. Then people were summoned from the set in the back lot and from the potting shed down in front, and eventually even the big shots joined in. But the weird thing about it all was that the cats didn't actually run away from the men who pursued them. Instead all they did was sort of circle slowly and warily around them and through them, moving quickly only when the men lunged at them now and then. And the men going after the cats also went around in slow circles, so that, to me, up in my window, it was a little like watching an eighteenth-century ballroom scene from above, with the dancers turning and wheeling and dipping in stately confusion.

In half an hour not one cat had been bagged, which led to some very worried looks on the faces of the big shots and everyone else, because the next day shooting was to begin.

Thirteen   MAY 4 dawned bright and clear. For me, things started off as usual, I got up fairly early, stumbled out to the kitchen, made a cup of coffee and took it into the living room. I noticed immediately that Chippy was staring intently at something outside, but at first I deliberately stayed away from the windows that looked out on the main set and sat down with my coffee to get myself together. But Chippy kept staring, and finally my curiosity got the better of me. I went over to the corner where her cage stood and saw something quite stunning. A very large truck—not as large as the General Camera generator truck out by the back gate but still very large—stood right outside Chippy's window, and when I say "right outside" I mean that somehow the driver of the truck had managed to back it along the driveway and snake it around the ficus tree and between the corner of the main set and the edge of the sunken garden and under the lower branches of the peanut-butter tree. The final result was that if there had been no screen in Chippy's window I would have been able to reach out and touch the rear end of the truck. But that wasn't really the alarming thing. The really alarming thing was that this truck, you could tell, wasn't just the kind of truck that carries something or other from one point to another and unloads whatever it is that it has delivered and then goes away again. This truck, by its levers and switches and gears and gauges and knobs and exhausts, was clearly the kind of truck that is equipped to perform some sort of industrial function, probably making a fearful racket while it is doing it. Whatever this truck's function was, I thought that it would have something to do with the big yellow accordion-type hose that emerged like a colossal caterpillar from the side of the truck, crept across the ground and disappeared into an opening in the rear of the main set.

I couldn't imagine how the truck could have come so close to my house without my having heard it, but there it was, and the only thing I could figure out was that I must have been sleeping like a rock when it had arrived.

I finished my coffee and got dressed and went outside. It was a little crowded around the bottom of my steps with all the cages and that huge new truck. Of course none of the cats were in the cages. They were all ambling around as usual, some aimlessly, some looking for a fight, some stalking lizards. I noticed that on the side of the truck there was a sign that said "Airconditioning Service." Putting two and two together, I realized that the function of the truck was to pump cold air into the interior of the main set so that the actors and the director and the camera crew wouldn't die of heat prostration. I knew that air-conditioning meant compressors and that compressors meant a lot of noise, and I wanted to find somebody to talk to about getting the truck moved away from my house.

I walked around to the front end of the truck and found a

man sitting in the cab reading a newspaper. He was a geezer. That is the best and truly the only way to describe him. Not an *old* geezer, just a *geezer*.

"Hello there," I began.

He didn't seem to hear me, even though I had spoken quite loudly.

"Listen . . ." I said a little louder.

He still didn't seem to hear me.

"Hey!" I yelled and waved my hands.

The man looked down at me quizzically.

"Huh?" he said.

"Listen, I don't want this truck so close to my house," I said. "I know there's a compressor back there and it's going to make a hell of a racket when you start it up, and I don't want to have to listen to it right outside my windows. Now, are you going to move this thing or do I have to go and get the producer and have him make you move it?"

"Huh?" he said.

I had a sinking feeling. The man was stone deaf, and he had probably gotten that way from hearing the roar of the compressor all the time, which meant that it was plenty loud.

"Nothing," I said.

I went around to the front of the main set. The first thing that struck me was the absence of the workmen who had been coming to the property every day for about a month. It seemed quiet without all their shouting and hammering and sawing. There was nobody around the set except a few technicians fiddling with some lights. I went on to the back lot and saw that the workmen's junker cars had been replaced by trucks from a catering service. One gang of men was busy erecting a huge striped tent, while another was unloading steam tables.

I drove down to the village with the intention of going to my mailbox and buying the morning paper and then coming straight home, but I decided to stop at the drugstore and have breakfast. I wasn't gone more than an hour, but when I returned the area near my back gate was a mob scene. Dozens of cars were pulled off to the side of the road, and people were walking along the road from their cars toward the gate. Traffic was backed up for a long way in both directions. A couple of motorcycle cops were trying to break the jam, but they weren't having much luck, so I just inched along like everybody else toward my own gate. When I finally reached the gate I saw that the whole back lot was full of cars and trucks and people, and I decided to go on past and circle the block and enter the property by the front gate.

I found the front gate not quite so heavily besieged, but instead of the usual familiar security guards a real policeman was on duty there. He didn't believe me when I told him that I lived on the property, and while we discussed the matter my car was blocking the road and a great honking of horns began. The noise grew louder and louder until a sergeant came down the hill and listened to my story, took my name, consulted a notebook and let me enter. I didn't have any trouble finding a place to park in the field because there were no cars or trucks at all parked down there. In fact there never had been. The reason was that ever since the movie people had arrived in force I had pretty much let the place shift for itself. I hadn't carried out any deadfall and I hadn't cut any grass, and so, things being what they were, the grass had grown quite tall and there were coconuts and palm fronds lying all over the ground. The workmen had taken one look at the height of the royal palms along the driveway and then at the size of the fronds that had fallen from them and they had decided that they didn't want to take any chances of having their windshields broken or their roofs caved in.

I drove between two royals and plowed ten yards or so into the field, first having checked the prevailing wind to make sure that my car would be parked in the direction away from where any fronds would likely fall, if they fell. Then I got out of my car and started walking up the hill, but just then a man came running down from the top of the hill, waving his arms frantically.

"Wait a minute! Wait a minute!" he shouted.

I stopped and waited for him.

"I'm Stu, the second unit director," he said pleasantly but wildly, puffing a little as he approached me. He had golden hair and big blue eyes and he didn't look more than twenty. "Listen, I'm sorry, whoever you are, but you can't park there. Your car is in the shot."

"What are you talking about?" I said, really beginning to feel impatient with the whole business. "The set's on the other side of the field."

"No, not the *gazebo*," he said. "This is the *driveway* we're doing now, and everything on both sides is going to be in the shot."

I looked beyond him up the hill and saw a camera up there with a crew gathered around it.

"Where can I park then?" I said.

Stu looked around wildly. "I don't know," he said. "How about somewhere out there along the road? I'm sure you could find a spot out there, and you'd be absolutely out of the shot."

"Listen, I live here," I said.

"You *what?*"

"I live here."

"You must be kidding," he said. "This is a location. These houses aren't *real*. They're just *sets*."

"The one back there behind the main set is real," I said, "and I'm not going to park my car out on the road. I'm going to park it somewhere within the boundaries of this property. Now where do you want it to be?"

"Why not in the back lot?" he said. "That's where everyone else is."

"It's full up," I said.

"Well, our gaffer will find a place for you, don't worry."

I had never heard anyone use that word before, and I wasn't even sure what it meant.

"Is that a promise?" I said.

"Listen, I'll go right back there now and tell him myself," Stu said.

"Okay," I said.

I waded back out into the field and got in my car and backed into the driveway, and then, as I turned and looked toward the road, I saw Frank Sinatra standing just inside the gate. He seemed to have come out of nowhere, and he was standing there all alone, going through a series of fascinating motions. I stopped, spellbound, thinking, There he is, in person, himself, the idol of millions, the King, the legendary Frank Sinatra. It seemed funny to see him all alone like that. You don't think of him as ever being alone anywhere. But it was his movements that truly captivated me. There he was in his Frank Sinatra snap-brim hat and his Frank Sinatra suit and he seemed to be practicing Frank Sinatra–ing! What else could it be? He would reach up and adjust his hat in the inimitable Frank Sinatra manner, square his shoulders à la Frank Sinatra, drag on his cigarette as only he would do it, take a couple of Frank Sinatra steps forward, sort of hitch at his waistline with the inside of his wrists in the familiar Frank Sinatra way, and then go back and adjust his hat and run through the whole routine over again. It didn't seem right somehow. In fact, it looked downright crazy to see him standing there Frank Sinatra–ing all over the place. The question was, why in God's name did Frank Sinatra have to Frank Sinatra? Outside the gate a lot of people had gathered and they were watching this strange performance too, but Sinatra didn't pay any attention to them or to me. He did his thing a couple of more times and then relaxed and strolled off into the field, toward the potting shed, or gazebo.

I watched him until he sat down in the shade all alone, and then I remembered Stu and the gaffer and I drove on down to the gate, waited for the policeman to stop traffic for me so that I could get out on the road, and then drove around the block and once more inched along toward the back gate. When I finally reached the gate a tall man in a white cowboy hat and boots and with a lean, powerful jaw and fierce eyes waved me to a parking place near the striped tent. I felt better then, rather as if I had been given honorary status as a movie person, and I even thought I saw people looking at me, imagining me to be someone of at least minor importance.

I strolled along the driveway, mingling with the crowd, and all of a sudden I found myself face to face with Frank Sinatra. A different Frank Sinatra! This one was standing in the sunshine, basking in the adoration of the small group around him, smiling, chatting, gazing coolly at the scene. He wore a light-gray suit with an enormous button pinned to the lapel that said "Italian Power." Actually, all of the people who were in his immediate vicinity were wearing

"Italian Power" buttons. I recognized two of them. One was Jill St. John and the other was Prince Michael Romanoff. I was struck by the difference between this Frank Sinatra and the other one. The one down by the front gate had been thin, sallow and nervous. This one was tanned and handsome, his compelling blue eyes full of self-confidence and good humor. This one obviously had no need to practice Frank Sinatra–ing, because to him it came natural. Someone came and whispered something in his ear, and he slipped away to a large silver air-conditioned trailer that was parked off all by itself under an oak tree.

I went on around the swimming pool and looked down the hill past the camera crew. The other Frank Sinatra, who, I realized by this time, was the real Frank Sinatra's stand-in, was at it again, standing all alone down there inside the gate, adjusting his hat, squaring his shoulders, dragging on his cigarette, taking a couple of steps and hitching at his waistline with the inside of his wrists.

Fourteen In the area of the main set there were a lot of big shots wandering around in the blazing sunlight with semi-hysterical looks on their faces, and I could hear them asking each other questions. One of the questions I overheard most frequently was "Listen, this is serious. What are we going to do about all these cats?" Then the person to whom the question had been addressed would say, "Yeah, what the hell are we going to do about all these cats?" But nobody did anything. They had apparently given up altogether on the cages. And the cats, realizing in their way that they had defeated the movie people, acted more snooty and regal and generally superior than usual.

I was standing in the driveway watching a group of technicians hard at work gluing a section of automobile-tire tread to the balustrade around the swimming pool and trying to imagine *why*, when all of a sudden I heard the air-conditioning truck start up with a great roar. I remembered that I had meant to ask someone to move the truck away from my house, but now of course it was too late. I hurried upstairs expecting to find Chippy going mad with fright. Instead she had simply gone into her house and curled up in such a tight little ball that she was barely visible. When I called to her she twitched and one eye appeared at a window for an instant. Then she went back to cover again. I closed her two windows, and that shut out the noise to a certain extent, and I directed a fan toward her house so that she would have a cool breeze to sleep by.

Outside, the crowd kept getting bigger by the minute, and I went down and sat on one of the benches by the pool. It was like a carnival, except that nobody seemed to be having a good time. Panic was in the air. It seemed as if everybody had lost something and was looking everywhere for it, or had been heartlessly betrayed by someone he had counted on, or had begun to feel inadequate and wanted reassurance. Meetings took place all around me, foreheads were slapped, hands fluttered helplessly, eyes rolled in resignation, shoulders were shrugged, mouths popped open in anger. Those who didn't look worried or morose or desperate looked unspeakably bored. The most bored of all were the young actresses who had been sent to the location by minor talent agencies to be discovered. At first I didn't know what they were all doing there, and I asked a very pretty blonde who came and sat beside me on the bench if she had a part in the picture.

"I wish I did," she said. "Then I'd be getting paid for wasting time like this. Is Sinatra here, do you know?"

"Yes, he's here," I said. "I saw him just a few minutes ago."

"Who else is here?"

"Who else do you mean?"

"The producer? The director?"

"I don't know."

"Do you know who the director is on this picture?"

"No," I said.

"I don't either," the girl said despondently.

She recoiled almost in horror when another pretty girl started to sit down with us. The other girl saw her and changed her mind and went away.

"The agency sent me here to be *seen*," the girl said. "So who's *looking?*"

I was looking.

She glanced at me. "Are you anybody?"

"No."

She shrugged. "That's the way it always is," she said. "The people you can talk to halfway like a human being are never anybody and the others won't even look at you. Where did you say you saw Sinatra?"

"Back that way," I said.

She stood up and touched her hair.

"Maybe I'd better wander back there," she said without much enthusiasm. She started to go and then came back. "Listen, thanks for the tip."

"That's okay," I said. "I hope he sees you."

"Yeah, whatever good that will do."

In spite of the apparent lack of organization and common purpose, I began to see that all of the scattered forces around the locations were actually working toward setting up a scene that was to be shot in front of the main set. Powerful lights had been arranged in a semicircle around the area, and two cameras had been set up, one close in and one farther back for long shots. Suddenly, in a blinding flash, the lights were all switched on at once. The sunlight itself was dazzling, but the lights outshone it, and when Frank Sinatra came outside and stood in the half-circle formed by the lights and the reflectors, he shimmered and glittered. There was a lot of noise, but when a man on a stepladder shouted, "Settle down everybody!" the whole location turned silent, and I realized that finally the filming was about to begin.

What I wasn't prepared for—what everyone is unprepared for who hasn't spent much time around movie sets—was the staggering tedium and frustration of shooting even

the most uncomplicated scene. All that was supposed to happen in this scene was that Sinatra was supposed to stand in front of the house and stare at it for a moment and then go cautiously up the steps, cross the terrace and go through the door. By the fifth or sixth take, my mind had begun to wander. The director, the star and the cameraman couldn't seem to agree on anything. They conferred, they agonized, they wheedled, they delivered ultimatums and then compromised. Finally they would all smile and slap each other on the back and try again. The man on the stepladder would shout for the zillionth time, "Okay, settle down everybody! Quiet on the set! This is a *take!*" And again it wouldn't be right.

I began to pay less and less attention to the shooting and more and more attention to the man who in the last analysis had been assigned to make sure the cats didn't come into the shot. This fellow had been given two pounds of chopped sirloin on a supermarket cardboard tray, and he was walking back and forth along the driveway holding the tray in one hand and with the other making the hamburger into little balls, which he tossed to the cats one by one. The cats followed him up and down on tiptoe with their tails sticking straight up, rubbing against his legs so passionately that he looked like a man wading hip deep in the surf.

Fifteen THE FILMING went on for four days and two nights. Late in the afternoon of the last day of shooting, Chippy was playing along the windowsill when she suddenly stopped and stood up on her hind legs. It always made me pause when she did that because I wondered what had caught her attention. I was sitting across the room from her, away from the front windows, reading a book or something, and I was about to go back to it when I saw her cock her head to get a better view of something down below her. In the old days, before the movie people had come and the place had been more or less my own private preserve, I had usually gone over to the window whenever Chippy had started ogling like that because it might have meant that somebody was walking around outside, which would have been something I probably would have wanted to investigate. But now that there were so many people around all the time, I seldom bothered any more. I was about to go back to my reading when I saw Chippy reach out one hand and rest it on the windowpane. This enabled her to lean over and get still better a view. At the same time she curled her other hand, which had been hanging limp, in toward her chest. Each of these movements of hers was an intensification of her posture of concentration, and the effect on me was like watching a person who is listening to someone tell him a long story over the telephone and whose eyes keep getting bigger and bigger while his mouth hangs farther open.

But finally I couldn't stand it any longer, and I went to the window and looked out. What I saw that was fascinating Chippy so much was Gordon Douglas, the director, and Frank Sinatra sitting together on a wooden bench below her window, discussing the script. They were alone. The rest of the movie people were out in the back lot. They had been shooting some scenes around the smaller set back there most of the afternoon. Douglas had a copy of the script open on his lap. I couldn't hear a word of what he and Sinatra were saying because they were talking in low voices. Anyway, it all looked perfectly innocent, and it seemed a shame that they couldn't even have a little private chat without being spied on by a nosy squirrel.

Chippy kept on staring, which of course was very rude, but I knew that it was useless to try to distract her because once she had gotten started on a really good stare the roof could have fallen in and she would have kept right on going. You would have thought to see her that she not only could hear every word the two men were saying and understand every word of it but that it was all of tremendous significance to her and possibly to all squirrels worldwide.

Sinatra reached into his pocket for a cigarette and a book of matches. Chippy's eyes sharpened. Sinatra put the cigarette in his mouth and struck a match, but it went out. Chippy leaned a fraction of an inch closer to the windowpane. Sinatra bent off another match and struck it. Chippy's whiskers moved. Sinatra lifted the match toward his cigarette, but before the flame touched the end of it he stopped. It was as if some thought had just occurred to him. For a moment he sat motionless, and then he raised his eyes slowly from the flame, which kept flickering a few inches from his cigarette. He turned his head and raised his eyes still more, all of this very slowly, until he was looking straight at Chippy's window. The match burned his fingers and he let it drop to the ground. He couldn't see me where I was standing, but I knew that he could see Chippy clearly because I had looked up at her many times from about where he was sitting and had seen her on the windowsill looking down at me. His eyes widened at the sight of the little figure gazing at him, and he was transfixed. He raised his hand to point to Chippy and at the same time turned to Gordon Douglas to tell him to look. But before he spoke to Douglas, who was still studying the script, he glanced up at the window again. Chippy had jumped over onto the table and disappeared from his sight. He blinked his eyes, let his hand fall, started to say something to Douglas and then just went ahead and lit his cigarette.

Sixteen   I wasn't around for the end. I finally gave up watching the shooting around midnight of the last day. They went on until about two o'clock. In the final scene that I watched, Sinatra had a fight with Shecky Greene by the swimming pool and ended up throwing him into the pool. The piece of rubber tire that had been glued to the balustrade around the swimming pool, it turned out, had been put there to cushion Sinatra's kidneys when he fell back against it and then flipped Shecky into the pool.

I went to sleep listening to the sounds of the crowd, to the loud intermittent buzz that meant that the microphones were open, the occasional bang of a pistol and the endless voice on the bullhorn saying, "Okay, settle down everybody. This is a *take*." I fell asleep and woke up a couple of times and still heard all that and saw on my ceiling the red light flashing from a police car that was in the last scene. When I woke up again it was terribly quiet. I couldn't hear anything but the wind in the trees, and I knew that it was all over.

The next morning I went outside early. The whole place looked other-worldly in the pale light. It looked as if everyone had just dropped everything and gone home right after the last take. The ground was covered with equipment and an extraordinary amount of litter. The enormous floodlights and the reflectors on their stands looked like robots hanging around waiting for somebody to program them to do something. There was no one in sight except a guard sleeping in his car near the main set and some men sleeping on the ground under the trucks in the back lot. A little later I looked out of my window and saw a couple of girls standing near the pool. They seemed lost, so I went out and said hello to them.

"Where's everybody?" they asked.

"I don't know," I said.

They looked heart-broken.

"Where's the director?" they wailed. "Where's the camera crew?"

"I don't think they'll be coming today," I said. "All the shooting is over on this location now."

"What are you talking about?" they said. "We're supposed to be doing a scene here this morning."

My heart sank. I had thought it was all over. I had been *promised* it was over.

"A what?" I said.

"A scene! A scene! And there's not even anybody here!"

Just then I saw Stu, the second unit director, coming along the driveway from the back lot. I went to meet him and said, "Listen, I thought you guys were finishing this thing up last night."

"Yeah, we made it," he said wearily. "We got the last take around two o'clock."

"Then what are these girls talking about?" I said. "They say they're supposed to do a scene here this morning."

"Take it easy," Stu said, grinning. "They're just going to do a bit down by the front gate. It won't take more than ten minutes. What are they doing up here anyway? The camera crew is waiting for them down there."

I felt better and watched Stu and the girls go down the hill. It really was all over. That afternoon the place was full of people again, but they were just technicians and workmen who had come to start packing up the equipment and cleaning up the grounds. The next day the workmen who had built the sets returned and began tearing them down. It always takes much less time to destroy something than it does to construct it, and it took only a couple of days for the three sets on the property to be reduced to junk and loaded onto trucks and hauled away. Finally one day about a week after the last day of shooting, the sets were all gone, the movie people were all gone, the cars and the trucks and the lights and the cables and the caterers and the tent and the guards and the portable toilets were all gone, and my little kingdom was tranquil again. It was as if the place had suddenly gotten tired of the whole thing and had sighed deeply and risen up like a big dog and shaken itself, and all the fleas had fallen out.

Of course, as I had suspected from the beginning, the land had not been left exactly as it had been found. The movie people had done their best to clean it up, yes, but it had been very severely trampled and would take a long time to recover. Trees were scarred, bushes were flattened, and the back lot on both sides of the driveway was a desert. Whenever I took a walk around I found souvenirs—bits of the orange celluloid that had been used as filters on the windows of the sets, sticks of hard black carbon that I think had something to do with the floodlights, plastic spoons and forks and hundreds and hundreds of nails. I remember an uncle of mine in New Hampshire who had put in a new lawn and had almost driven himself to distraction trying to pick all the pebbles out of the soil. I picked up nails from the grass around the sets endlessly, and when I thought that at last I had found them all I would always find some more.

At first it was hard to get used to the idea that I was alone again, just as in the beginning when the movie people had first come it had been hard to get used to the idea that I wasn't alone any longer. And you can get used to a structure being in a certain place very quickly. For a few days it gave me a start every time I looked out my window and didn't see the main set there. When I went outside I automatically walked around the set, though there was nothing left of it to go around but the large rectangle of yellowed grass where it had stood.

I bought a long hose and stood for an hour or so every day watering the dust in the back lot, because the weather continued dry and I was afraid the whole place would blow away if I didn't keep it soaked. I started cutting the grass again and hauling out the deadfall to the road. I began hoping the foxes would return to the property now that it was safe again, and I walked around calling them and left eggs and water in the old places, but I didn't see them. A couple of times I even went across the road to the field by the bay and looked for them. I saw a man shooting at gulls with a .22 and plenty of shell casings lying on the ground, but no foxes.

Gradually I stopped being so depressed and unhappy with myself, and the feeling that I had to leave the house and my squirrel and my book behind me and go out into the world and start a whole new life passed away. Chippy and I began to have good games again. One day I took the cover off my typewriter and went back to work on my novel.

Part Three

Seventeen　THE OUTSIDE world kept closing in steadily that summer. The new buildings continued to rise up above the trees to the south, the sounds of heavy construction advanced, the cars flew past on the roads in increasing numbers and the trucks going by all day shook the ground. The rifles kept firing away at night too, although I often wondered what there was left by now for them to shoot at.

I never stopped worrying about the foxes. I kept chicken necks in the freezer for them, and I always searched the ground for signs of them when I was out walking. I would have given anything for even a glimpse of the kits playing again, but then I imagined that if they were still alive at all they weren't beautiful and carefree any longer but had probably taken on the dead-tired and desperate look of their parents. Whenever I drove along the road beside the field next to the bay I was afraid that I would see one of them either squashed on the pavement or lying like an old gunny sack in the weeds on the shoulder. I didn't, but I saw plenty of other furry bodies, squirrels, raccoons and, more than anything else, opossums.

Opossums, I'm sorry to say, are one animal that I have never been able to relate to. In fact, for reasons that are not entirely clear to me, I actually dread them. Therefore, it was not with great joy that I noticed that summer that the property had begun to attract opossums in fairly large numbers. Of course I felt sorry for them, and I never would have dreamed of trying to chase them away. I knew that they were under terrific pressure from encroaching civilization just as the foxes and the raccoons and all the other animals were and I was very sympathetic. I wished them the best, all the luck in the world, but I also wished they would go away. I would see them at all hours, in the early morning, in broad daylight, at night, and they always made me wonder. How had they been able to make it all these eons? They moved so sluggishly, they climbed so awkwardly, and, honestly, they seemed to have absolutely nothing going on between their ears.

I remember going outside one day and seeing a couple of them standing around in the field. They didn't seem to have anything much on their minds, and when they saw me coming toward them at a distance they ambled off toward the trees. Although it was really the last thing on earth I wanted to do, I followed them. They kept looking back over their shoulders at me to see if I was following them seriously, and when they saw that I was they ambled a little faster. Finally they disappeared into the bushes under the oaks, and I could hear them crashing around in the dry leaves back there, about as stealthy as giraffes. I kept on after them, fully expecting that by the time I reached the trees the two opossums would have gone so far back into the underbrush that there would be no question of my getting close to them, but when I got there and peered into the bushes I saw them standing right near me, gazing at me with curiosity.

It was the first time I had ever been face to face with an opossum, and I'll say this: They don't look anything like Pogo. These two were, I assumed, full grown. At any rate they were about as big as medium-sized poodles. I think that I had hoped when I had begun to follow them that if I could get up close enough to have a good look at them, perhaps I could lose my fear of them, but it didn't work. There was something about those white faces, those little eyes, all those teeth and those naked tails that looked sort of like long pink carrots that chilled me. So we just stared at each other for a while, and then I went my way and they went theirs with nothing at all accomplished in the direction of better understanding of each other.

And it didn't help either when I went to the library and read up on opossums. Their whole life style sounded

vaguely creepy. The thing that baffled me most about them was the fact that they were tree animals to begin with. How had it come about? No animal in the world seemed on the face of it to be a more likely candidate for an entire existence spent with its feet planted firmly on the ground, because when you thought of a tree animal you thought of something light and swift and agile. What I'm saying is, it is one thing to "swing" through the trees like monkeys, or to "race" or "fly" or "sail" through them like squirrels, but to "lumber"? It didn't seem right somehow. And I had a good many opportunities to observe this lumbering. It began to be not unusual for me to look out of my window and see an opossum walking by above me, because the branches of many trees touched the steeply slanted tile roof of the house. It had become a matter of habit with the squirrels to use the roof as a regular part of their highway-in-the-sky system, jumping out of a tree and onto the roof on one side of the house, running over the roof and flinging themselves into a tree on the other side. Now the opossums had started copying them. I would see something move above the rain gutter, and a moment later an opossum would step off the roof onto a branch of the sapodilla tree. After having gotten so used to seeing the squirrels do it—all in quick, nervous leaps, a flash of white underbelly fur, the tail twirling like a propeller— seeing an opossum in the trees was like seeing a pony. They moved hesitantly and unsteadily along the branches, always looking as if they had never been in a tree before and really couldn't imagine how they had managed to get themselves in a fix like this. Yet, amazingly, they never fell, and slowly but surely got where they were going.

The secret of their survival as a species, I suppose, is that they reproduce copiously. They will eat just about anything in a pinch and live just about anywhere, and though they may climb awkwardly, they can make their way to a hiding place high up in a tree when they have to, which, one must admit, is more than a fox can do for all his quickness and his beauty and his bushy tail.

While I was seeing more than I really wanted to of the opossums, I wasn't seeing nearly as much as I wanted to of the raccoons, although there were plenty of them around. I often saw them prowling in the neighborhood of the sunken garden at night, and once I saw a whole family of them playing for a few minutes in the bright moonlight down on my terrace. But that wasn't enough. I knew several people who complained that raccoons were "pestering" them—always hanging around by the kitchen door looking for handouts, knocking over garbage cans, raiding their goldfish ponds. I wished some raccoons would pester me. I had read and heard enough about them to know how intelligent they are and how fascinating to watch, and of course I think that it would take a hard heart indeed to be able to resist their charming little masked faces. I thought it was unfair that they wouldn't pester me. I really felt discriminated against. And it didn't seem to me that I was asking too much. I wouldn't have tried to make pets of them. I wouldn't even have invited them into my house because I knew that Chippy probably would have been very stuffy about that. All I wanted was for them to regard me as a friend and to feel that they could hang around outside my kitchen door all they liked. I did everything I could think of to attract them, even going so far as to try to send out positive vibrations saying, "All raccoons welcome here." But it didn't do any good.

The only time I had a chance to get close to a raccoon

was one afternoon when I was walking along beside the
hedge down at the bottom of the front field next to the road
by the bay. I happened to spy an animal with a pair of shiny
black eyes gazing at me from deep back in the pine needles.
It was a small raccoon, probably about a year old. He didn't
seem to get alarmed when I stopped and he knew that he had
been spotted, but just kept sitting perfectly still in a crotch
of the hedge that was on a level with my eyes. It was around
five o'clock. I imagined that he lived in the mangrove trees
by the bay and had come across the road the night before to
forage and now was waiting patiently close to the road for it
to get dark and the heavy traffic to slacken off so that he
could go back. I knew that he had a long wait ahead of him,
and I thought he must be hungry and thirsty, so I ran back
to my house and looked through the icebox for food that I
thought would appeal to a raccoon. I finally selected a chunk
of Muenster cheese and a knockwurst. I filled a small saucepan
with water and was about to go out the door when I
remembered that raccoons like to wash their food before
they eat it, so I went back and filled a bigger saucepan with
water. I couldn't run going back down to the field because I
would have spilled the water, but I walked as fast as I could,
hoping that the raccoon wouldn't have gone away.

When I reached the hedge I found that he was still there
but had climbed into a crotch that was a bit higher up than
the other one. First I held the pan of water up to him,
pushing it through the twigs. He didn't seem to be the least
bit afraid of me, and when he smelled the water his nose
twitched. Reaching down eagerly, he took hold of the rim
of the pan with both hands and stuck his nose in and had a
long drink. When he was through drinking I found a stick
and put the piece of cheese on the end. Then, holding the

stick in one hand and the pan in the other, I pushed them both up through the foliage toward the raccoon at the same time so that he could wash the cheese in the water if he wanted to. He took the cheese and wolfed it down, showing not the slightest interest in washing it first, and then he had another long drink of water. He didn't wash the knockwurst either, which made me wonder about all those stories I had heard, but wolfed that right down too and then had still another long drink.

The cars going by made a frightening rushing sound, and when trucks passed the wind from them swept along the hedge in violent gusts. But the raccoon seemed calm. He was very handsome and great fun to watch, but I knew that animals don't like to be stared at, and after a while I returned to my house. I went back down to the hedge later on, when

it was getting dark, and I was just in time to see the raccoon climb down from his perch and run along the ground at the base of the hedge. Soon I lost him in the fading light. There were fewer cars going past by then, and I assumed that he was getting ready to cross the road. I often looked for him after that in the hedge, but I never saw him again.

The only thing that worried me about the presence of all the raccoons and opossums on the property was the possibility that a mated pair of one tribe or another might discover the cave in the sunken garden and move in and set up housekeeping. I was hoping that in the fall the foxes would come back to the cave and have their new babies there. However, I really had nothing to worry about on that score, as I was to find out one morning about a month after the movie people had left.

That morning I went out as usual at about ten o'clock to distribute sunflower seeds around the bases of eight trees along the driveway. I had started putting out the seeds right after the movie people went away as a gesture toward letting the squirrels and the birds know that things were getting back to normal and we had the place all to ourselves again. I had thought that I would do it just for a couple of days, and in the beginning I had put the seeds only around the base of Mother Squirrel's palm tree. Mother Squirrel was a big, tough female who was the undisputed boss of all the squirrels in the territory around the sunken garden. I called her Mother Squirrel because I had always rather thought that she must have been Chippy's mother. She had her nest in a coconut palm directly across the driveway from the cave in the sunken garden, and it was from that general area that the cat had come loping with Chippy in her mouth.

Mother Squirrel had two batches of babies every year as

regular as clockwork, one in the spring and one in the fall. Sometimes there were two and sometimes three. I always got my first look at the new babies when Mother Squirrel brought them for the first time to the peanut-butter tree. I would go out on the balcony to put the peanut butter in the peanut-butter tree, and there they would be, the proud mother and two or three mice beside her on the limb. Squirrels are never again quite as beautiful as they are in their first fur. Their tails are never again quite as light and perfectly shaped nor their fur as silky. The proud father was of course not really very proud, couldn't have cared less, in fact, about the whole deal and was nowhere to be seen. I was pretty sure I knew who Mother Squirrel's mate was, though, a male I often saw around the garden. I called him Trouble because every time I saw him he was either chasing another male squirrel, being chased by Mother Squirrel or looking as if he was on his way to pick a fight somewhere. I could tell Mother Squirrel from the other females because she had a little notch in her right ear, and I could tell Trouble from the other males simply because he was much bigger than any of the other squirrels. In fact, for a gray he was gigantic. However, gigantic or not, he didn't impress Mother Squirrel, and when she chased him he ran squealing and chirping.

Anyway, in the beginning I had just scattered a handful or so of seeds around the base of Mother Squirrel's palm tree and she had come down the curving trunk, which was etched with the claw marks of generations and generations of squirrels, with her newest babies. They had all sat around cracking the seeds in a neat and orderly way, and if the blue jays and cardinals swooped in and stole a stray seed now and then, that was all right too. But then, as time went by, the minute I went out and stood in the driveway and started beating on the side of my two-and-a-half-pound plastic bag of sunflower seeds to call Mother Squirrel down from her nest, squirrels began running toward me through the trees from all over the place. That was bad because naturally Mother Squirrel felt that she had to defend the seeds from all comers, which was really more than even she could handle, and it got so that she spent so much time chasing after and nipping the bottoms of the invading squirrels that she never got any of the seeds herself. By the time she came back to the base of her tree her babies and the birds would have finished them all off.

So I had begun putting seeds around the base of an iron-wood tree across the driveway from Mother Squirrel's palm tree. That had worked for a couple of days, but then more squirrels had started coming. The quarreling had begun again and had gotten so intense that I had finally decided that the only way to solve the problem was to keep the squirrels as widely separated as possible, with the result that I had soon found myself putting equal amounts of seeds around the bases of eight different trees along the driveway. That was how the ten-o'clock distribution of the seeds, which had started out as a gesture, became an institution. But I must admit that there was something in it for me too, because every morning after I had strewn the seeds I stood still in the driveway and listened, and fifteen squirrels at the bases of eight trees all cracking sunflower seeds at the same time is one of the most endearing sounds I have ever heard.

On the morning I'm talking about I had just gone out to the driveway and was about to start thumping my bag of seeds to summon the squirrels when something made me stop. I looked behind me and saw the male fox. He was standing near the entrance to the swimming pool, at a particular spot where I had often seen him before, just where the driveway began to curve around the pool, near a jardiniere filled with ferns. It gave me a funny feeling to see him there. It was like turning around suddenly and seeing someone you haven't seen in a long time staring at you and sensing that he has been staring at you for a long time, waiting hesitantly for you to turn, too shy to come up and speak to you himself. Now his mouth opens slightly and his hand is half raised as he wonders if you will recognize him and greet him, or not recognize him, or recognize him but choose to cut him dead.

Of course I was terribly happy to see him. I know I smiled and started to go toward him, but then another feeling came over me, an undeniable premonition that something was very wrong, and I paused.

He was standing out in the full morning sunlight and I could see him clearly. It was him, there was no doubt in my mind about that, the little father fox, but there was something about him, the way he stood, the way he kept gazing at me, that was so unlike him that he not only didn't seem like himself but not like a fox at all. He could have been anything—a rather scruffy little reddish, grayish dog, a stuffed fox, anything but a real fox—and the feeling I had was that he had come to tell me something that I didn't want to hear, and it was very strong.

So I stopped, and when the fox took a step toward me I took a step backward. He came forward again, a few steps, into the shadow of the ficus tree, and I moved away from him, slowly, always going backward to keep my eyes on him, and he came after me, just a few steps at a time. What I really wanted to do was turn and run as fast as I could around the garden and up the stairs to my house, but I had truly begun to believe that the fox would run after me and attack me if I did that. Instead I edged my way around the garden, stumbling over some fallen coconuts, being brushed across the back by vines, passing in and out of shade and sunlight, watching the fox coming along uncertainly after me. Finally I came to the foot of the concrete pathway that led from my house to the back field. From there it wasn't far to the house. I stood still and watched the fox come closer, and the closer he came the less I felt that he was a threat to me. He walked very stiffly. He looked sick. When he came within about ten yards of me he paused and turned himself sideways to me, and I saw that he had taken a load of buckshot in his right flank at fairly close range.

When I had seen it, he settled down on the grass with his paws tucked under him and his head held erect. I sat on the edge of the barbecue pit that stood at the foot of the path and stayed with him that way for about ten minutes. Then I went upstairs and got a pan of water and two eggs. I put the water and the eggs down on the grass near the fox, but he didn't look at them. He stood up and started walking across the field toward the oak trees, and I followed him, carrying the water and the eggs. He had to lie down and rest several times, so it took us a long time to reach the trees. When he went into the trees I didn't try to follow him any farther. I put the eggs and the water at the place near the pond where I had always left his food before. The next morning some of the water had been taken, but the eggs were still there. The morning after that neither water nor eggs had been taken, and when I started to walk down the driveway toward the front field there was a sudden horrible flapping of wings, and a great black bird rose up swiftly out of the trees. Then I looked up and saw three or four other buzzards circling low above the trees, and I knew that it was all over.

Eighteen

I FOUND lovely Billy Blue Jay one day in mid-June. I went out to the garbage can and saw him on the grass on my way back. If I hadn't happened to look right at him I never would have seen him, because he was being very still and quiet and he wasn't as big as a minute anyway. Seeing him made my heart sink. I knew that I would have to do something about him, but my record at saving birds, going all the way back to my childhood, was so miserable that I almost thought that wherever they were and whatever shape they were in when I found them they were better off than they would be in my tender care. At least they could just expire with dignity and without all the inconvenience of having some stupendous clod manhandling them and trying to force food down their throats.

He was just a tiny ball of light blue and gray-and-white fluff. When he was sure that I had seen him he cocked an eye at me defiantly. I looked up at the oak tree spreading above him. It was one of the big ones that grew out of the sunken garden. I could see the nest that he had fallen from

clearly. It was lodged securely between two thick philodendron vines that were entwined around a limb, and it was an
excellent place for a nest because it was protected from rain
and sun and owls and hawks and everything else by the large
philodendron leaves that formed a canopy over it. I looked
for the mother bird but didn't see her anywhere, and there
were no other small birds in the nest. It was still early in the
afternoon, and I knew that if I left the little blue jay alone
his mother would probably come and feed him, but I
couldn't do that because I also knew that at any moment one
of the cats might come along and find him. As a matter of
fact, I had seen a tom prowling not too far away when I had
gone to the garbage can.

So I squatted down and talked to Billy for a minute, to let
him see that I was a friend, and then I picked him up. I had
expected cries of alarm, but he didn't struggle or fuss at all,
and I cupped him in my hands and took him upstairs.

I had left Chippy playing in the living room when I had
gone out with the garbage. As soon as I went back inside the
house with the blue jay I looked around for Chippy, and as
usual I couldn't see her anywhere. I was walking around in
circles, looking under things and calling her name, when she
suddenly jumped onto my shoulder from the top of a high
cabinet, startling me so much that I almost dropped the little
bird. I had been calling her just so this would not happen, so
that I would know where she was and she wouldn't be able
to jump on me or run up my leg unexpectedly and then run
down my arm to my hands to find out what I had cupped
between them. I knew that she would be beside herself with
excitement if she discovered that I had brought a bird into
the house, and I was afraid that she might frighten Billy to
death if she sneaked up on him for a close look.

Naturally, the first thing she did after she landed on my shoulder was to run down my right arm toward my hands. Billy's head was sticking out from between my hands, and Chippy wanted to sniff him, which was exactly what I didn't want her to do. Since I was helpless, with my hands full, and Chippy wouldn't pay any attention to me when I yelled at her to keep away from the bird, I did the only thing I could think of on the spur of the moment to try to make her go back up to my shoulder. I started dancing around in exaggerated waltz steps, the theory being that usually when I started doing something crazy like that Chippy would run up to my shoulder, figuring that it would be most prudent to get to high ground right away and determine if this monkey business might be dangerous or harmful to squirrels in any way. And it worked. After I had made a few graceful swooping, sliding turns in the middle of the room, Chippy ran up to my shoulder and froze there. My next move was to try to get her to jump from there onto something else, and the way to do that was to bring my shoulder suddenly in close to something like the back of a chair. Squirrels were brought into this world to jump, and their instinct is always to jump to something else if there is anything else near enough to jump to. So I started darting around the room, bent over like Quasimodo, throwing my shoulder at windowsills, backs of chairs, tables and ledges, but Chippy wasn't buying it. Instead of jumping she began running all over me excitedly, and since all I had on my back was a tee shirt, she was flaying me alive. Also, I was pretty sure that Billy Blue Jay wasn't enjoying the whole show too much either.

Finally I faced up to the inevitable, that Chippy was going to get a sniff of the bird no matter what, and I went into the bedroom and knelt down beside my bed. Then I rested my hands on the bed. Chippy had run down to my left wrist and was gazing at Billy intently. Billy was gazing back, just as intently, but he wasn't afraid. He was accepting the situation just as it was, wasn't asking any questions, wasn't laying down any conditions, just trying to be nice and get along with everybody. But Chippy couldn't get over it. We had never had a bird in the house before. What a development! She pulled her tail around in front of her eyes, a battle tactic used by squirrels that combines the advantages of both a shield and a smokescreen, and advanced half an inch on Billy behind that great bush. Then she suddenly retreated a full two inches and stood there, giving Billy what baseball pitchers call "a lot of motion," which means that they flail their arms and legs around a good deal just before they deliver the pitch to try to distract the batter and make him swing too early or too late. She lurked behind her waving tail, peering through the guard hairs with one wary eye at the small face poking out from between my hands, bobbing and weaving, sometimes even breaking into the squirrels' war dance, a rapid drumming of the back feet. I think Billy was saying to himself, "Well, I certainly didn't ask for all this, but if this is what you have to put up with around here, this is what you have to put up with." As for Chippy, I wished that I could have told her that I had brought her into the house in similar circumstances not very long ago, so don't get too smart.

In the end, since it had begun to look as if this program was going to go on forever, I did what I often had to do when Chippy was too chicken to run in and take a sniff of something on her own. I lifted my right hand from over Billy and gave it to Chippy to sniff. She sniffed it passionately, in the squirrel way, pecking at it rapidly with the tip of her cold wet nose. Usually when I had to perform this little service for Chippy it was because she had gotten herself into a swivet over some totally innocent object that she didn't quite like the looks of. For example, if I let her out of her cage and carried her across the room on my shoulder and sat down on the couch to give her a squirrel brushing and she happened to see something suspicious at the other end of the couch—such as a magazine, some crumpled paper, a shoelace—then she would feel compelled to go into her act with the tail and the drumming because she could not feel safe until the offending object had been identified and found harmless to squirrels. So rather than sit through the whole boring performance, Chippy trying to surround a shoelace, I would reach over and take the shoelace between my fingers, rub it a couple of times and then give my fingers to Chippy to sniff. The instant she knew it wasn't alive she would relax, and she was perfectly shameless about it because she would never let on that she had been scared of the shoelace or whatever it was to begin with. She would simply dismiss the entire affair with a grand flick of her tail, and if you didn't start making yourself useful with the squirrel brush right away you were asking for a medium to hard nip on the thumb.

Once Chippy had had a whiff of Billy from my fingers she seemed to think that that was enough for the moment, and she ran up to my shoulder to wait and see what would happen next. I took my hands away from Billy altogether, and there he squatted on the bed, looking around at everything curiously. He didn't mind when I examined him to see if anything was broken. Luckily, he was completely intact. He even stood up on his matchstick legs and spread his wings for me. When he did that I noticed that there were parts of his scrawny little body under his wings that weren't even covered with feathers yet, so I knew that he really was still an infant. I picked him up and set him on the forefinger of my left hand. He clamped onto it securely, and the three of us, the squirrel on my shoulder and the bird on my finger, went looking through the house for a small box that would make a good nest for Billy. I found exactly what I was looking for on a shelf in the kitchen and stuffed the bottom of it with strips of newspaper. Then we all went back into the bedroom and I put Billy into his nest. I had a hard time making him let go of my finger—he could really hang on with those little talons of his—but as soon as he had settled himself in the box he didn't seem unhappy.

I went back to the kitchen and made a little supper for Billy of bits of hamburger and mashed apple and banana all mixed together—a formula that I remembered having read somewhere that was supposed to be suitable for young birds—and filled an eyedropper with water. But before I could return to the bedroom, Chippy insisted on smelling the concoction I had whipped up for Billy. Needless to say it wasn't anything that a squirrel would like, since they never eat meat in any way, shape or form, and so then she had to put on the big display that she always did when she wanted to get it across to me that she didn't approve of the way something smelled. She started wiping her nose and mouth on my shirt, rubbing vigorously for a minute in one place and then moving onto a fresh place and rubbing again, as if my shirt was nothing more than a gigantic squirrel napkin. She kept it up for such an unnecessarily long time that I wanted nothing so much as to give her a good pinch. It was all so overdramatic and exhibitionistic—and the worst part was that neither her nose nor her mouth had ever touched the despised mess in the spoon. It was just the very smell of it that she was trying to expunge. On top of that, nobody had ever offered her any of it to begin with, so what difference did it make whether she liked it or not?

I finally returned to the bedroom with Chippy hanging by her hind feet from the back of my collar, still wiping her nose on my shirt, and I knelt down beside the bed again. This was the crucial moment. I had never had much luck in the past with getting the birds I was trying to save to eat anything, so they had all died. But one thing that rather encouraged me now was the fact that Billy was a well bird, whereas all of the other ones I had had experience with had either been hit by cars, chewed up pretty badly by cats or had broken a wing or a leg. Furthermore, I had had such great success with bringing Chippy through from infancy that I felt that maybe I was on a winning streak.

I put a tiny glob of food on the end of the eyedropper and brought it up close to Billy's nostrils. Then I began trying to get him to open his bill, which he was extremely reluctant to do. I was getting nowhere and beginning to feel nervous when all of a sudden his bill flew wide open and I was gazing down a pink throat that looked about the size of the Grand Canyon. I quickly stuck the food down his throat, added a squirt of water to help it on its way and got the eyedropper out just before the bill clanged shut. It flew open again an instant later, and this time Billy broke his silence with an authentic hungry baby-blue-jay heart-stopping earsplitting shriek. Of course I had been hearing those shrieks for years around the doughnut window, but I had never had one go right off in my face before, and the effect was quite stunning. It even got a reaction from Chippy, who had been trying to sneak up on Billy again. She ran to my shoulder and stood up very straight and tall in the squirrels' attitude of superwariness. I kept shoveling the food down Billy's throat as fast as he would take it, and he kept shrieking at me at the top of his lungs. But I didn't mind, because I thought that if he could yell like that and eat like that he certainly was going to make it.

Nineteen

I COULDN'T help wondering if Chippy would be jealous of Billy and might try to hurt him. I had nothing to go on in this respect because Billy was the first animal visitor we had ever had in our house—except for the hamster, and he had lasted only about half an hour, so I didn't think you could really even count him. The hamster was a perfectly amiable little gentleman I had picked up in a pet store one day when Chippy was still a very young squirrel, thinking that she ought to have a pal to play with. I had brought him home and put him in the bottom of her cage, and then I had called her. She had been napping at the time, but in due course she had emerged from her house to see what was going on, had taken one look at the creature bumbling about among her possessions down on the floor and had gone back to bed in a huff. I got the message and returned the hamster to the pet shop and asked the owner to be sure and try to find it a good home.

But Chippy didn't show any signs of jealousy, even when

I took Billy out for walks, which was something he enjoyed immensely. I would stroll all over the property with my handsome blue jay perched on my right forefinger, and he would be as quiet and as good as an angel as long as I kept walking. However, the instant I stopped he would start wailing at me for something to eat.

It seemed that there was no satisfying him. He was hungry all the time, and all I had to do was look at him and his mouth would fly open and he would wail and flutter his little wings at me. I kept feeding him the mixture of apple and banana and hamburger that I had had luck with in the beginning, and I also gave him an occasional bit of sunflower seed. I thought that was all right because I had often seen the mother blue jays popping sunflower seeds down their babies' throats. My main problem was that I didn't know how much I should be feeding Billy or how much water he was supposed to be drinking. I was pretty sure that I was feeding him too much, but I kept remembering articles I had read about birds having to eat enormous quantities of food to stay alive. I couldn't remember the figures exactly, though. Twice their own weight every hour? Ten times their own weight twice a day?

After the first couple of days I began to wish that Billy would try to feed himself, because I thought he would know best how to regulate his intake. I put him down on the floor in front of food and water and refused to feed him for several hours, but he wouldn't even peck at his food or touch his water, so I had to go back to feeding him rather than let him starve. I wondered how long I would have to go on feeding him. I had a feeling that it was going to be quite a long while, because one thing I had always noticed about blue-jay babies was that they seemed to want to stay babies longer than other birds. I would see a new batch of cardinals around the doughnut window, and it seemed that within a few days they would have stopped begging from their father (it is the male cardinal that feeds the young) and would be stuffing themselves with doughnuts on their own. However, with the blue jays the begging went on and on, with the result that I was always being treated to the spectacle of two or three huge babies all lined up on the trellis and begging mercilessly at a mother blue jay, who was so thin and nervous from rustling up food for them from dawn till dark that they looked twice as big as she did. But the mother never seemed to think that there was anything ridiculous about the situation and flew wearily back and forth between the doughnut window and the trellis, stuffing the gaping mouths that were always waiting there for her.

Sometimes one of the babies would go in for the drooping-wing trick, where they would hop around on the trellis with one or both wings dragging behind them. They were trying to get across the idea that they were so weak from hunger that they couldn't even pull their wings up, I guess, and as corny as it was the mother would almost always fall for it and feed that baby more than any of the others. Blue-jay babies are so shameless that they will even beg from each other when there aren't any mothers around. I would see one of them land on the doughnut window, look around quickly to see that he wasn't being observed by his mother and start gobbling up doughnuts as if there was no tomorrow. But when another baby would land beside him he would immediately stop eating and start begging from his sibling, who would be doing exactly the same thing to him, and they would both stand there in a sea of crumbs with their bills wide open, wailing pitifully. And when the mother finally arrived to see what was wrong with her darlings they would stop panhandling each other and turn on her together. You could imagine the sort of splitting headache the poor old thing would go to bed with every night.

I loved my Billy, but I was determined to return him to the wild as soon as I could, before he drove me and Chippy out of our minds. When he wasn't begging from me, he turned to Chippy, who simply didn't understand. She wanted to be a good sport about it. She would even try to entertain him sometimes, but he didn't understand that either. While she lay on her back in front of his box, kicking her back feet in the air and swishing her tail for all she was worth, he would stare at her with his head cocked to one side, and his blue jay's frown, which was formed by the black lines between his eyes, would become particularly intense. Then she would get up on her hind legs and hold onto the edge of his box and dance, but the minute she paused the mouth would fly open and the wailing would begin.

I thought the best thing to do was to keep Billy outdoors as much as possible, so he would get used to being with his own kind. So I would put Chippy's cage down on the terrace every afternoon and then go and sit with Billy on the steps or on the glider. It always seemed that not long after I went outside with Billy several big blue jays would start gathering around me. I would look up at the oak tree and see two or three of them gazing down at me. Then one of them would swoop down and land on the trellis or on the dough-nut window or on the light standard, making a soft whistling sound. After a while another jay would come down lower, and they would all sit around me and make the whistling

sound together, as if they were in conversation around a sickbed. I realized that they were interested in Billy and I had the feeling that they wanted to get close to him, but I was afraid to leave him alone with them because of something that had happened about a year before involving a red-bellied woodpecker. I had found the young woodpecker by the road just after he had been knocked senseless by a car. I had taken him home and examined him and had thought at first that he was just stunned and would recover in due time from the accident. His wings and legs were intact and he hadn't lost very many feathers. I thought that all he needed was rest, and I made a little nest for him in a hanging basket that hung from a limb of a small pine tree over the back railing of my terrace. It was cool there, and for a while he seemed quite perky with the breeze blowing over him and all the birds coming around to keep him company, but then suddenly a male and a female red-bellied woodpecker arrived and began making quick passes at the bird in the basket. It was obvious that they were trying to kill him, so I went and got him out of the basket, but then I noticed something about him that had escaped me before. He couldn't hold his head up straight. He tried but it kept lolling to one side. When I saw that I realized that the two woodpeckers had known that the little bird's neck was broken and that he could never survive, and they were right because it was only about an hour later that he died.

However, one afternoon when I was sitting on the terrace with Billy the phone rang. I put him on the bottom of a small cardboard box and went inside. I could look down into the box through the window as I talked on the phone, and I hadn't been in the house more than two minutes before I saw a blue jay fly down and land on the edge of the box. I was going to run out and chase her away (I assumed that it was a female, although with blue jays it's hard to tell), but I decided to let nature take its course. I hung up and stood at the window and saw the blue jay hop down into the box with Billy and move in a circle around him, and I guessed that she was looking him over to see if he was healthy. Then she flew away, but she came back a moment later with something in her mouth. She hopped into the box again and stuffed whatever it was she had brought him into Billy's mouth, and then she flew away and did the same thing over again. I let her make the trip three times before I went out and got Billy out of the box. I had noticed that he hadn't wailed even one time at the blue jay, but he took right up where he had left off wailing at me as soon as I had him sitting on my finger again.

After that I began taking him down to the front field in the afternoons, and I would put him on a leafy twig of the melaleuca tree and then go off a short distance and sit on the grass to wait and see what would happen. Sooner or later a couple of blue jays would come and sit in the branches above Billy, and one after the other they would fly down and put food in his mouth. He was a good boy and he let them mother him, but I had a strong feeling that he didn't relate to them or to the trees and the clouds and the sky and the great outdoors in general. What he really seemed to relate to was Chippy and me and my house, and I didn't think that he ever wanted to leave. He always refused to beg from the blue jays, but he continued to wail at Chippy and me endlessly. He also didn't seem to want to learn how to fly, and I thought that perhaps he saw that Chippy and I didn't fly, so why should he?

I tried my best not only to teach Billy to fly but also to

interest him in the whole glorious idea of flying, but he was suspicious. Most of the time he withdrew into himself and refused even to spread his wings, much less flap them.

I would hold him about a foot above my bed and then pull my finger out from under him, and he would drop like a dead weight. I would "fly" him around the room by making my finger dip and rise. In order to keep his balance he would have to open his wings, and in spite of himself he would sometimes have to fly a little way. But what he really liked to do was hop around on the floor after Chippy and me, bawling for attention. This distressed me because I thought it would never end, and it distressed Chippy because what *she* really liked to do was slip through the house like a phantom, silently and mysteriously, and how could she do that with a loudmouthed bird always hopping after her? Once in a while, when Billy got to be too much for Chippy, she would opt out of the situation by going up to her house and blocking the door with her tail. This would shut out the sight of the bird and the sound of him too, I guess, leaving Billy down on the floor, alone, perplexed and frowning worse than ever.

I don't remember exactly how long all this went on, but it seemed like a very long time, and then one morning Billy's instincts got the better of him. I took Chippy out on the terrace in her cage that morning and then came back up and got Billy. It was a particularly fine day, and the terrace was alive with birds eating doughnuts, looking for bugs in the hanging baskets and the bougainvillaea and splashing in the birdbath. Actually, at that time the terrace was just getting back to normal after a nasty week or so during which Molly Mockingbird, who had her nest in a jasmine vine near the terrace and who was usually the picture of good manners,

had suddenly gotten it into her head to "take over" the doughnut window and then had proceeded to do so. It was a painful and embarrassing experience for everyone, and it almost killed Molly. She posted herself at the window early in the morning and was on guard without letup all day. Not one bird or one squirrel did she allow near the window. In fact, she wouldn't even let the birds come to the birdbath. Finally, of course, she burned herself out. Her awful compulsion passed, and she went to her nest and rested for a few days. When I saw her again she looked like someone who had gone to the end of the night. But, really, the less said about all that the better.

This fine morning I was called into the house for some reason. I put Billy into the cardboard box as usual when I went inside, but when I came out a little later I found the box empty. I couldn't believe my eyes. Billy had never even tried to get out of the box before, and the truth was that the only way he could have gotten out was to have *flown* out. I looked around for him, and on all sides of me there were blue jays, all looking one exactly like the others. I realized what had happened. Billy had seen all the birds flying

around him and had been overcome by an urge to fly, and once he had flown he had passed over onto the side of the birds and had become a part of their world and couldn't come back to ours. I called to each of the blue jays and stuck my forefinger toward them, but none of them looked at me in a more familiar way than any of the others. They could all have been Billy or none of them. Perhaps, I thought, he wasn't even near the terrace now but was far away somewhere testing his marvelous new wings. For a few minutes I was stunned at the loss of Billy and how quickly it had come about, but then I began to feel very happy for me and for him because the story had had such a perfect ending.

Twenty   On DAYS when the heat was almost unbearable
in the house I wished that I could take Chippy outside with
me, because there we're certain places on the property that
were always cool. I imagined the two of us sitting side by
side on a bench in the deep shade about halfway up the slope,
whiling away the afternoon gazing across the road at the
blue bay.

But I was afraid to take her outside unless she was in her
cage, because I didn't know how she would behave. Or,
rather, I knew my squirrel all too well and I was positive
that she wouldn't behave at all, that she would last about one
minute sitting with me on the bench and then would want to
be off exploring in the trees, and that would be the last I
would see of her.

But one day I decided to take a chance. At least, I hoped,
we could take a short walk outdoors. So I went to Chippy's
cage and called her. On days like that she slept most of the
time, but in a most unsquirrelish position. Normally she
curled up in a ball in her house. In the heat she lay on her

back with her head sticking out of her doorway, the back of her head resting on her porch and her nose sticking straight up in the air. Sometimes I would turn a fan on and direct it toward her house, and then she would go into her house and curl up (and, I think, sleep more comfortably), but I didn't like to do that too much because I had read that small animals are extremely sensitive to drafts.

When I called Chippy she had no idea what an adventure I had in mind, and I had a hard time getting her to come down. Finally I bribed her with a piece of saltine cracker. She had recently become very fond of salt and couldn't resist it when I opened the box, crackling the wax paper, and snapped off a piece of crisp saltine. I gave her time to eat her bit of cracker, sitting on my shoulder, and then I opened the kitchen door and went outside. I had picked what I thought was an ideal day. There was no wind to speak of. All was calm and quiet. My plan was to go only a short distance and to walk pretty fast so that Chippy would stay up on my shoulder. My experience had been that when I was walking around in the house with her on my shoulder, she would stay up there as long as I kept moving, but when I stopped she would run down my leg to the floor.

I thought that the most difficult part of the trip would be passing under the trellis, because Chippy would be tempted to jump either to the bougainvillaea or to the trellis itself. I went down the steps to the terrace, ducked low as I went under the trellis and then hurried down the last steps to ground level. No problems. I walked along the driveway past some cats, who paid no attention to me, and then set off across the field toward the oak trees. This was the first time Chippy had been outdoors outside of her cage since I had let her go. I could feel her excitement. When I looked from the corner of my eye at her, I could see her straining toward the oak branches ahead of us. But I never came close enough to them to make her think of jumping. Before I reached the trees I turned around and went home.

Back in the house Chippy went into her cage and stretched out on a branch. I could tell that our walk had given her a good deal to think about.

The next day I took her for another walk. This time we went farther. In fact we went as far as the back gate. Just to see what would happen I paused a couple of times, and Chippy immediately started to run down to the ground, so I began walking briskly again to make her go back up to my shoulder. On the third day I took her down to the front field, where she had never been except for once or twice when she was a baby squirrel and I had taken her for walks tucked into my shirt pocket, but of course she couldn't have remembered that. She was impressed by the coconut palms and the royals and the huge kapoc trees, and even when I stopped she stayed on my shoulder and smelled the wind from the bay.

It was on the fourth day that these little walks of ours suddenly turned into one of my greatest squirrel crises. The evening before I had swept some leaves together at the bottom of the steps and had forgotten all about them. Then, the next afternoon, when I carried Chippy down the steps I stepped right into the middle of this pile of leaves. Of course leaves are a vital part of a squirrel's warning system out in the woods. When they hear the slightest rustling in the leaves they stop whatever they are doing and listen, and Chippy, even though she had lived her whole life indoors, was just as sensitive to the sound of leaves as any wild squirrel. Therefore, when I stepped into the pile of leaves she was so alarmed by the loud crash I made that she sprang a fantastic distance from my shoulder to the trunk of the sapodilla tree. It was a truly remarkable leap, and for one or two seconds I couldn't really believe that Chippy could have made it. But there she was, clinging to the trunk. I went over to her right away, feeling that I was going to have just one chance to get her out of that tree. I stuck out my elbow toward her and said, "All right, come along, Chips," in a medium stern voice. She gazed at me, and for a moment she almost fell for it, but then it occurred to her that there she was, as free as a bird, and she tore up the trunk as far as the first branches.

I began to feel quite disturbed. I had played my best and only card with no result. How was I ever going to get Chippy home again? And to make matters worse, it was very late in the afternoon of a day that had been heavily overcast since noon. In no time the light would start fading away altogether.

Chippy came down the trunk a little way, and I tried the voice and the elbow again, but there was no result. She looked at me, hanging upside down by her back claws. When I moved closer to her she scooted around the trunk, hiding from me, being very playful. "Squirrel-in-the-tree" in real life. When I went around the trunk after her, she shot up to the first branches again. And then something happened that made my heart sink. Another squirrel appeared in the branches above Chippy. Then another. And another. There were squirrels all over the place. Of course! That sapodilla tree at the foot of the steps also happened to be the peanut-butter tree! Mother Squirrel and her babies, plus Trouble and all of the other squirrels that lived around the sunken garden, were coming over to the peanut-butter tree to see if

I was putting out peanut butter for them. All of a sudden a squirrel's face appeared looking at me around the side of the trunk, very close to me. I said, "Okay, Chippy, the fun is over" and jogged my elbow right in the squirrel's face. The squirrel stared at me, and then I realized that it wasn't Chippy. Another squirrel appeared near me. Was it Chippy or wasn't it? They all looked so maddeningly alike! And they kept running down and looking at me and then running back up into the tree while I tried frantically to study their faces.

At that point another disastrous thing happened. A girl I knew arrived in her car, parked in the back lot near the barbecue pit and came strolling happily along the path toward me. I signaled to her to stop, but she didn't understand, and it was too late anyway. The path was full of unswept-up leaves, and her feet crashing through them had already caused all of the squirrels to run high up into the tree.

I went over to a bench and slumped down disheartenedly. When the girl asked me what was going on I told her the whole story and she felt miserable. I told her it wasn't her fault. But she was disconsolate.

"Is there anything I can do to help you get Chippy back down?" she asked.

"Nothing," I said. "Nothing, nothing, nothing. Nothing. I think the ball game is over."

Just then I heard a couple of squirrels chasing around up in the sapodilla tree. It was a sound I knew so well that at first I didn't even bother to look up—just Mother Squirrel chasing one of the other squirrels out of the peanut-butter tree. But then I did look up just in time to see the squirrel that was being chased hurl itself from a branch of the sapodilla tree onto a nearby branch of one of the big oak trees in the garden. Both squirrels began racing around in the oak tree at blinding speeds. There was a good deal of squeaking and squealing and squirrel growling, and from time to time the gap between the two of them closed and I knew that Mother Squirrel must be getting in some darned good nips. As the disturbance continued, I began to listen more closely to some of the squeaks. While it's true that all gray squirrels look more or less alike and their squeaks all sound more or less alike, these squeaks sounded very familiar to me. I got up and went to the base of the oak and looked up again. The two squirrels were swirling around and around the trunk about twenty feet above me. Abruptly, the one that was being chased broke away and headed straight down the trunk toward me. I knew what was expected of me and held out my arm, and with Mother Squirrel not two inches behind her Chippy made a desperate leap and landed safely on my forearm.

I marched her upstairs on my shoulder and she hopped into her cage. She was a much chastened squirrel, and after it was all over and I had time to think about it I realized that I wasn't the least bit sorry that it had happened. I thought of all the times when Chippy's impossible behavior had made me wish that I could give her a good nip, and it seemed to me that Mother Squirrel had gotten me even finally.

Not long after this episode I had another bright idea. For a long time I had had my eye on a certain coconut palm down in the front field, thinking that it would be an ideal tree to turn Chippy loose in for a little afternoon's outing. The reason it was ideal was that it was one of the few trees on the property that stood completely alone. No part of it touched any other tree, so Chippy would have to stay in it and wouldn't be able to wander off wherever her curiosity led her. I waited for a quiet afternoon and carried her in her cage down to the front field, which was a tremendous task in itself—but after the experience with the peanut-butter tree I didn't trust her to stay on my shoulder any more. The coconut palm I had selected stood about in the middle of the field. It was a tall palm that leaned toward the north. The curve of the trunk was so long and gradual that you could run almost halfway up the trunk barefoot without having to use your hands. Up at the top was a huge tuft of fronds with many coconuts hanging below them. I put the cage down right next to the trunk, with the door in a position so that Chippy could hop right out onto the trunk.

When I opened the door Chippy came out immediately and got on the trunk and started climbing slowly. Halfway up the tree she stopped, smelling the wind and looking at the cars going by on the road. She stayed there, clinging motionless to the trunk for rather a long time, so I sat down on the grass, leaned up against the trunk of a royal palm and started reading the paperback book I had brought with me. When I looked at Chippy again I saw that she had climbed a little higher. It took her about twenty minutes to reach the top of the tree, which was not at all what I had expected. I had thought she would be very excited and would do an enormous amount of running around.

I watched her climb into the crown of the tree, and I could see her smelling and investigating, but not too clearly because she was high up off the ground now. Soon she disappeared altogether into the crown, and I went back to my reading. I kept looking up from time to time but I couldn't see Chippy at all. What on earth was she doing up there? I wondered. I got up and walked across the field to get a different view of the crown of the palm. From there I saw Chippy just for a moment, when she came a little way out on the trough of a frond and then ran back into the dark brown and green and yellow mass of the crown.

I sat down and read a while longer. Then I went around the field collecting deadfall and carried it out to the pile by the road. By then Chippy had been in the tree for more than two hours, and I was beginning to get a little bored with the adventure.

I called her, cupping my hands to my mouth to make sure she could hear me, but nothing happened. I sat down again, read a little and watched the birds in the field. Another hour went by, and then as far as I was concerned it really was time to go home. I stood up and called Chippy again, this time more seriously, and walked around under the tree, trying to see where she was hiding. I couldn't see a trace of her. I kept walking around and calling, and then an awful suspicion began to come over me that perhaps while I had been reading Chippy had sneaked down the tree and run to another tree and by now was off, who knew where? I was sure it couldn't have happened, and yet it was the only thing that seemed to make any sense. Suddenly feeling panicky, I ran back up to the house and got my field glasses. Then, peering up through the glasses at the crown of the tree, I walked all over the field, looking at the tree from every possible angle. I was about to give up and assume that Chippy really had sneaked down and run away when I spotted a familiar tail hanging down between two fronds high up at the very top of the crown. I could never have seen it from any angle with my naked eyes, but with the glasses I could see it quite clearly. It was blowing gently in the wind.

Then I understood what must have happened. Chippy had simply found a comfortable bower in the top of the tree and had settled down for a good long snooze, out there in the sunshine and the fresh air, high up where she knew she was absolutely safe from Mother Squirrel and everyone else and so could feel that she was the queen of everything.

I just couldn't think what to do. I was tired of being down in the front field. I was *very* tired of straining my eyes and craning my neck and walking around and yelling. I was impatient to get that squirrel back into her cage and back home. But how was I going to get her down, short of climbing up there and grabbing her, which I wasn't about to do anyway, since I am deathly afraid of heights?

Another miserable half hour went by, and I was beginning to talk to myself in my frustration. However, as I was pacing up and down my eyes happened to fall on some baby coconuts that lay on the ground under Chippy's tree. They were about the size of golf balls, and it occurred to me that it might shake Chippy up a little if I could hit the crown of the tree with one of them. My trouble was that I can't throw. I have never been able to throw snowballs, baseballs, spitballs, anything. All I could hope for was that if I hit any part of the crown it would get results.

So I wound up and let fly, and the baby coconut seemed to go astonishingly true to its mark. There was a sudden movement in the tree, and I grabbed my glasses and saw that where there had been a tail hanging down before there was now a small and, it appeared to me, outraged face poking out between the fronds. Although it was hard for me to believe that I could have made such a shot, the facts seemed to indicate that I had hit Chippy squarely on the rump!

She was annoyed. She had probably never had such a

lovely nap in her whole life, and to be awakened so rudely! So she took her own good time about coming down. She did it by inches, in a long spiral down the trunk of the palm. It was getting late and she was hungry for her corn or it would, I'm sure, have taken even longer. I scolded her when I finally got her into her cage, but she was still half in dreamland and didn't pay much attention.

Twenty-one   ON A very hot morning in early July
Chippy attacked me. The attack came as a sickening surprise because we had been getting along very well together
for many months. In fact, it was the first time she had attacked me seriously since she had come back from the woods.

I was sitting on the couch in the living room, holding some
pecans in my right hand, when it happened. Chippy had
been coming and getting the nuts one at a time and dashing
away to hide them all over the house. Her mood had been
playful, but suddenly it had changed and she had begun
running around the living room very fast. She had run faster
and faster, in circles on the rug. Then she had widened her
circle and started running underneath the furniture, under
the chairs and tables, disappearing under one end of the
couch and shooting out the other end an instant later like a
little toy train out of a tunnel. Finally she had jumped up
and begun running *over* the furniture, leaping from chair to
table to couch, and this had indeed been a frightening exhibi-
tion because she had had to fling herself recklessly across

some quite wide spaces. She had had a most purposeful look on her face and had never slowed down or shown any signs of getting tired, and I had watched her with growing alarm. I had known what all this portended. I had seen it before. It was like a war dance in which the warrior works himself into a frenzy so that he can attack his enemy with complete abandon and utter ferocity. I had been afraid to move, because I knew that in this context the slightest movement on my part was considered a provocation. So I had sat there with the pecans in my hand, covered with a light film of perspiration from the unspeakable humidity that saturates south Florida at that time of year, and hoped that something would distract my squirrel and make her forget about biting me.

But soon she jumped down to the floor again and began to run at my legs repeatedly, dashing toward them and then swerving away at the last moment and kicking out at them with her hind feet. The claws on her hind feet were terribly sharp, and each time she struck me she slashed me through my pants leg. This was the start of an attack. She was trying to get me to make a move that would give her an excuse to go for me with her teeth. When I remained still she attacked me anyway, biting me first on the hand that held the nuts and then, so quickly that I hardly knew what was happening, on my left arm. At that I leaped to my feet, scattering the nuts all over the room. Chippy sprang at me and tried to bite my right hand again, but I shoved it into my pocket. Then she ran off a little way to collect herself for another assault, and I retreated toward the nearest door, which happened to be the door to the bathroom. Chippy ran at me again but changed course at the last moment and hopped up onto the back of a chair, and I slipped through the door.

When I poked my head out ignominiously, I saw my squirrel perched on the chair, clicking her teeth and waiting for me to dare to come out.

The humiliating truth was that this wasn't the first time I had taken refuge from Chippy in the bathroom, and as I stood in there it occurred to me that the other time had been almost exactly a year before. That day she had attacked me suddenly and without provocation too, and I remembered my blood on the doorjamb. She had hit me worse that time. I had bled all over the place. I turned on the light and looked at my wounds. My hand was bleeding freely, but although the bite on my forearm was deep it wasn't bleeding at all. I washed the blood off my hand and examined my arm under the light. The puncture was turning blue, and a small hard knot was rising under the skin. I touched the knot and wondered what it meant. None of the many scratches and bites that Chippy had given me in the past had ever become infected, and none of them had ever caused any swelling either. I sat down on the toilet seat, feeling very discouraged. It wasn't the blood and the pain and the swelling that bothered me so much. What bothered me was the fear that the awfulness was starting over. Did this attack mean that the whole cycle of surprise attacks and clicking of teeth and growling and the maniacal defense of her nuts that I had gone through with my squirrel the year before—and which had led finally to my decision to put her out in the trees—was beginning again?

When I looked out into the living room again a few minutes later I saw that Chippy had gone back to her cage, which was her normal procedure after she had attacked me and I had hidden from her. I crossed the room and closed the gate and fastened it securely, while she watched me closely, lying motionless on a branch. It looked as if she was wondering if I had learned my lesson now. What lesson? What had I done wrong? The last time she had chased me into the bathroom I had lost my temper and clapped my hands at her when she had gone back into her cage. It had scared her badly because I had never done anything like that to her before, and it had been a pretty cowardly thing to do. She had run around in her cage hysterically for a long time, and I had just hoped that she wouldn't hurt herself. This time I didn't do anything to her. Actually, I didn't even feel angry with her. I just said, "Bad girl, Chips" and went and got a drink of cold water from the icebox.

The knot on my arm began to look worse, so I thought I had better go and show it to a doctor. I had to walk down to the village because my car wasn't feeling well that day, and since I didn't have an appointment at the doctor's office I had to sit around in his waiting room for quite a while before he saw me. Doctors frighten me even when they're cheerful, easygoing souls, but the ones who keep me waiting a long time and then act cross on top of it scare the wits out of me. This doctor was very gruff and rough. He had no time or sympathy for minor things like squirrel bites. He wasn't the least bit impressed with my knot and dismissed me with a shrug and a tetanus shot.

I went back out into the stifling heat, feeling a little better because I wasn't going to die but still depressed about Chippy's attack. I walked to the garage where my car was getting fixed to see how things were coming along. My car was still up on the rack, but the mechanic told me that if I wanted to wait around for a few minutes he was almost finished. I waited, and when he was writing up my bill he noticed my arm.

"How did you get that?" he asked.

I told him the story, and while I was telling it he gazed at me steadily without saying anything. Then he took the money I handed him and went over to the cash register to make change. On his way back he kept on gazing at me, and when he handed me my change and I took it he still kept on gazing. He had the sort of eyes that look at you so intently and unblinkingly and directly that just looking back into them is a terrific challenge and gives you a slight headache, and yet you can't evade them. To look away from them, you can't help feeling, would be a defeat and would also probably have some kind of deep meaning that you would rather not think about. The truth was, with those eyes he was crazy to be a mechanic. He should have been a revolutionist or nothing at all. So he kept on gazing at me, with a red-and-blue-tipped wooden match between his teeth. I knew he was going to say something I wouldn't like, and even though he took forever coming to it and I had to keep popping my eyes to keep from blinking or looking away, I waited patiently, because a good mechanic is hard to find nowadays and there are things you just have to put up with from them sometimes whether you like it or not. In other words, you have to show them some respect. This is the price of good timing and proper carburetion.

"You know what I would have done if it was me?" he said finally.

I knew better than to answer. A rhetorical question is a rhetorical question no matter where it comes from.

"If that was me and that goddam squirrel had bitten me like that, I would have taken him—"

"Her," I said.

"What?"

"You would have taken *her*," I said quietly but firmly. "She's a female."

"I don't give a goddam about that," he said, intensifying his gaze a little. "This is what I'm saying. If that had been me and that goddam squirrel had bitten me like that, I would have taken him by his goddam tail and this is what I would have done. I would have swung him around my head a couple of times and then I would have let go and splattered his brains all over the side of the goddam house. Because there's no goddam animal of mine that's going to turn on me and get away with it. And that goes for if it's a dog or a cat or even a goddam *horse*."

Driving home, I thought about what the mechanic had said, and I had to admit that, although perhaps too strongly expressed, his attitude was basically correct. One should *not* let an animal that lives in one's house and eats one's food attack one and get away with it. Okay. Very true. Very nice. Very simple. But granting all that, how do you apply the rule to a squirrel? A squirrel is a very different sort of thing from a dog or a cat or even a horse. You can't exert your will over squirrels the way you can with other animals. I had tried scolding Chippy—she had just ignored it. I hadn't tried spanking her—that surely wouldn't have done anything but guarantee a hard bite for my trouble. It would be useless to withhold food from her—she had her own supply in her house and could hold out indefinitely if it came to that. So what would the mechanic do in my place? Of course what he had really meant was that an animal should understand who's boss from the very beginning. You should get that idea across clearly at the start, and that having been settled, then the question of an attack should never come up—and if it does the animal knew all along that there would be consequences and therefore can't complain one bit if it gets its brains splattered all over the side of the house.

When I got home Chippy bounced around in her cage, begging to be let out. She wanted to play, of course. That was the way it always was. She got the meanness out of her system and then she wanted to forget all about what had happened and thought I should too.

I paid no attention to her and went and sat down and felt sorry for myself. The thing is, I'm just like everybody else. When I sweep a problem under the carpet I expect it to stay there and not come popping out again at the worst possible moment. I didn't want to deal with any problems of any kind right then. Life had just begun to return to normal at this point, about two months after the movie people had decamped. Everything was gradually getting back to being calm and quiet and regular and smooth and controlled, as it had been before they had come. I was working hard on my book and was beginning to get back some of the confidence in its viability that I had to have in order to go on. I just wanted to be left alone and continue with my work—and now here was Chippy again.

As I said earlier, when Chippy had begun attacking me the year before, I had taken it to mean that in her own way she was telling me that she wanted to be let go. Now I thought about that again, and then the guilt that I had always felt started nagging me again about having kept her past the time in the beginning when she was old enough to be set free and by all rights should have been. I brooded all afternoon but didn't get anywhere or come to any conclusions. Or rather, I finally decided to let things ride for a while and see what happened, which was the sort of non-decision I was famous for and which almost always turned out to be a serious mistake. But, I persuaded myself, perhaps this attack hadn't had any deeper meaning. Perhaps it was after all just an isolated event and not at all the first drum roll in the onset of a situation as impossible as the one of the previous August and September.

So, in the end, I let Chippy out of her cage, and since it was getting on toward evening by then and she was naturally fairly docile around that time of day, I sat down on the couch and waited to see if she would do what she usually did. As I had expected, she came humping across the floor toward me, climbed up on my knee and lay stretched out flat in her accustomed way, facing away from me, her chin resting on my knee, her back legs straddling my thigh and her claws hooked backward into my pants leg, wanting her brushing. I reached over to the end table near me and got her squirrel brush (which really was an old toothbrush with a fairly stiff bristle that was perfect for the job) and started brushing her. To brush a squirrel properly you should take hold of its tail with one hand and grasp it firmly. This keeps the squirrel from sliding forward when you make your long strokes against the fur from the base of its tail all the way up the back, between the ears and then on down the nose. Also, it keeps the squirrel from pulling its tail protectively up over its back while you're brushing (it's purely a reflex action on their part) and getting it in the way of your strokes. You should take particular care with the thick fur around the base of the tail, which has a tendency to mat because the squirrel has difficulty reaching that area with its teeth to comb it out. They like to have their noses brushed, and they will obligingly close one eye at a time while you're doing it. They also like to have the thick fluffs of fur at the backs of their hind legs combed out, and for this, if they're in a good mood, you can lift them gently by their tails, thus raising their rumps a few inches off your knee so that you can bring your brush into play. Generally, it's a fine idea to start off by brushing against the fur for a good long while, raising the nap and pulling out loose hairs, and then to finish up by laying the fur down again with smooth strokes from the nose back to the base of the tail.

While I brushed I glanced occasionally at the bluish knot on my left forearm, and I couldn't help wishing that there was some meaningful way that I could convey to Chippy the seriousness of her having hung a thing like that on me, but there wasn't, so I just kept on brushing until she started rolling half over on her back to play with the brush. Then one thing led to another, and soon we were engaged in a full-fledged game of squirrel-in-the-tree, and while that was going on I thought of my mechanic again and wondered what he would think if he could see me now.

Twenty-two   We all spend most of our lives hoping for the best, and, as we all know, sometimes it works and sometimes it doesn't. In this case it didn't. Only a couple of weeks after Chippy had attacked me and given me the knot on my arm, she attacked me again, just as savagely. The circumstances were about the same. I was holding some of her hard-shelled nuts in my hand, and she was coming and getting them one by one and running away and hiding them. Then she got wound up and started running around the room very fast and suddenly bit my hand three times.

And then soon after that, one dark day in August, she began the annoying and depressingly sad business of clicking her teeth and growling at me whenever I came near her cage. This was the same thing she had done the year before that had almost driven me out of my mind and had contributed enormously to my final decision in September to take her out and put her in the trees. It meant that she was defending her supply of hard-shelled nuts both inside her house and on the floor at the bottom of her cage. Squirrels click their teeth rapidly as a preliminary warning. Their growls (which come out sounding like a low moan) are more serious and are meant to be taken more seriously. They mean "One false move and I'm going to be all over you."

Besides the nerve-racking aspects of the clicking and the growling, it was also difficult for me simply to get used to Chippy making any sound at all. Normally she was absolutely silent, except for the rare times when something outside upset her and she started making the *chuk-chuk-chuk* that everyone who has squirrels in his backyard has heard from time to time. It was almost always male cardinals, their color and their call, that brought this on. The only other time I heard anything out of her was occasionally in the middle of the night when she was having a bad dream and would let out a high piping cry. That, if she kept it up long enough, got me out of a warm bed to go and stand by her cage and stick my hand in her box to let her know that I was there and it was just a dream and everything was all right.

But the nerve-racking aspects of all the clicking and the growling were formidable. Chippy watched me constantly and took every move I made as a threat to her precious hard-shelled nuts, no matter how slight or insignificant it was or how far away from her across the living room I happened to be at the time. And when I approached her cage she would spring at the bars like a tiger, with a peculiar, deadly glint in her eyes. If I moved around the cage she would pursue me, springing at the bars time after time and trying to reach out at me through them to rake me with her claws. I couldn't stand near the cage very long because if I did she would stop striking at me and go into a frenzy of running up and down. She would run down to the bottom of her cage to check on all of the nuts hidden in the little holes she had scratched out of the newspaper on the floor and then run full speed back up to her house to go in and check on all of the nuts hidden *there*, and then back down to the floor, on and on and on. It was not only alarming to watch her, but also I was afraid that she might go into some kind of a fit of hysteria and injure herself somehow if she kept it up too long.

When I wanted to clean her cage in the morning I had to put on my gloves. When I stuck my fingers through the bars of the cage to lift it she would usually make one quick fake pass at the leather and then run up to her house to watch me from the doorway, growling ominously. I picked up her cage and moved it out of the corner, and then I took up the newspaper on the floor, revealing the glorious collection of nuts that my squirrel had hidden in the holes in the paper. The big dilemma was what to do about these nuts. Give them back to her or not? I wanted her to have the nuts because I considered them an essential part of her diet. I knew that the diligent gnawing that she had to do on them in order to open them was vitally important. A squirrel's lower teeth never stop growing, and if they are not worn down by continuous gnawing on something they will eventually grow so long that the squirrel will die of starvation because it will not be able to eat anything at all.

On the other hand, since it seemed obvious that the nuts were the root of the whole problem, wasn't I simply contributing to Chippy's delinquency when I put the nuts back into her cage after each cleaning? Shouldn't I have kept them from her and in that way steadily reduced her store of nuts? The mathematics of it was on my side. She usually ate one or two hard-shelled nuts a day over and above her regular ration of corn and lettuce, etc. She had, all told, I estimated, roughly twenty nuts of all kinds in her house (she slept on them, which was about the equivalent of sleeping on a mattress of cobblestones for you or me), and she had something like half a dozen more nuts hidden in the newspaper on the floor at any given time. It had been my custom to pass out to my friend about a dozen nuts a week at the rate of two or three a day (sometimes more, sometimes less) while she was out of her cage. Of these, part would be hidden here and there throughout the house and part would be taken to her cage. Of the latter, some would be hidden in her house and some on the floor. It should be clear by now that I was dealing in fairly large numbers of nuts when you remember that this was going on week after week and month after month, but I could well afford to do it because the previous fall and winter I had laid in a large supply, having found out to my alarm that fresh-in-the-shell nuts are generally not so easy to come by in stores in south Florida in spring and summer. I kept this wealth of pecans, walnuts, brazils, etc., on a shelf in the bathroom where Chippy could not possibly get at them, because I knew that if she could have gotten at them she would not have rested until she had robbed and hidden every one.

But to return to my math, if she had about twenty nuts in her house and I took away the ones on the floor and didn't give her any more and she used up the ones she had at the rate of about two a day, it followed that pretty soon she would be all out of nuts. This was also, of course, provided that I didn't let her out of her cage at all during this period, because God only knew how many nuts she had hidden all over the house. They were behind the books, under the rugs, stuck between the cushions on the couch and the chairs, in the piano, in my shoes, among my manuscripts, in the flower pots, under my typewriter, back of the phonograph —everywhere. They were also, alas, in all of the closets. Chippy would sneak into a closet when I was off guard for an instant and a door happened to have been left open, even though she knew that all of the closets in the house were strictly off limits to squirrels. She would hide a nut in there, and then that would be that, because once a nut was hidden someplace she remembered it forever and had to go back to check on it, so all she did was wait for the next opportunity to get back into the closet to see that her treasure hadn't been fooled around with. And, I assure you, there is no end to the trouble a squirrel can get into in a closet. Aren't there always things in every closet that are just waiting to be pushed over and knocked down?

There was one closet in particular—I suppose everyone on earth has one like it if the truth be known—into which I had the very bad habit of simply tossing things that I wanted not to throw away exactly but just get out of my sight. Over the years this closet had gradually gotten so stuffed with junk that finally it had reached the point where I opened the door quickly and shot something in and then had to push it closed against the avalanche. I really hadn't the remotest idea what all was in that closet. A band of gypsies could have been living in there the whole time and I wouldn't have known it. The worst thing about the closet was that its door had been cut a size too small at the bottom, which meant that there was just enough space for a squirrel to squeeze under, with a walnut in its mouth. I had made a baffle of a piece of cardboard held in place by a wastepaper basket at each end to keep Chippy out, but you can't always remember to put something like that back in place after you've removed it for some reason, any more than you can always remember to keep all the closet doors closed all the time. So Chippy would get in there and the crashings and the landslides would begin, and it was almost impossible to get her out. In the first place I never could see her when I looked in. Hell, I couldn't even see her half the time when she was right out in the open in the living room, the way she blended into the background, whatever the background happened to be. I had to stand there with the door only a little way open, peering into the darkness, holding back the piles of junk, calling Chippy in hopes that she would move so that I could see her and tell her about all the terrible things that were going to happen to her if she didn't come out right away. Finally she would usually appear high above me on a promontory, looking down at me. How she had ever gotten up there one would never know, but in her heart she knew how wrong she was, and after a moment's hesitation she would jump onto my shoulder.

Anyway, the point is, to make the nut-depletion scheme work, Chippy had to be kept in her cage and not allowed to roam around the house at all, which was profoundly against my principles. I had never wanted her cage to be an actual cage. All it was supposed to be was her own special part of the house. I couldn't even bear to look at caged animals in a zoo, and just the thought of caging such a gloriously free and wild thing as a squirrel was to me immensely saddening.

But I decided to try locking Chippy up for her own good. The only trouble was, she seemed to guess immediately what was up, with the result that she just stopped eating nuts altogether. Morning after morning I checked the newspaper at the bottom of her cage to see if there were any cracked shells scattered around or if she had hidden any nuts intact in the newspaper, but I never found anything. She was making it on corn and lettuce and all of the other perishables that I gave her every day, and she was damn well keeping her nuts safely up in her house in case of an emergency. When I caught on to what was happening, I still kept her locked up, but I went the other way completely. I started inundating her with nuts. I laid enormous quantities of nuts on her, covering the floor of her cage with them and in that way trying to demonstrate to her very graphically that not only was there no danger of a nut shortage but that I was being as open-handed with them as anyone in his right mind could be. But that didn't do any good either. The old confusion, the old mixing up of the giver-of-nuts with the taker-of-nuts syndrome had set in again like ten tons of cement, and she ran at my fingers just as fiercely when I was shoveling the nuts in to her through the bars as she would have if I had been trying to sneak them out.

I guess I tried everything at one time or another. Once in a while I would get so exasperated with Chippy and so tired of her clicking and her growling that I would lower the beach towels that covered the top of her cage and let them hang down all the way around so that the whole top part of the cage was shrouded and I couldn't see her when she was up in the top part and she couldn't see me. But anyway, behind the curtains I could hear her clicking and growling monotonously away, and she knew that I could hear, so what good did all that do? Then, other times, I would take her down to the terrace in her cage, hoping that out there with the birds and everything to distract her she would leave off the unpleasantness for a little while and that perhaps that might break the habit. But she didn't pay any attention to the birds any more. All she had on her mind was her pecans and cashews.

One day, near the end, when I just couldn't stand any of it any more, I decided to raid Chippy's house and take every nut she had to her name away from her. In order to accomplish this I dressed up in one of the most extraordinary costumes that has ever been devised. I blush when I think of it, even to this day, but it seemed absolutely necessary at the time. First I put on two long-sleeved shirts, then two pairs of pants, then a terry-cloth robe, and then I took a towel and put it over my head like a monk's hood and wound it around my neck so that there was just a little of my face showing. And *then* I put on the pigskin gloves.

When Chippy saw this apparition coming toward her cage she couldn't believe her eyes. She knocked off all of the sound effects and just stared. When I opened her cage she came inching over toward me on one of her branches, her eyes glittering with apprehension, her great gray bush of a tail fluffed out and hooked around in front of her eyes as a shield. She hadn't been out of her cage at all in a long time, so I stepped back, knowing that she would want to come out, and she came out and climbed down to the floor and started mousing around. When she had moused all the way over to the far side of the room, I took off my left glove and reached up into her house and began taking out her nuts and stuffing them into the pocket of my robe. The instant Chippy heard what I was up to she came dashing toward me. She leaped at my robe and ran up to my shoulder and was going to spring at my bare hand from there, but before she could do it I whirled around, shoved my hand into my pocket and walked quickly into the bedroom, carrying her with me. For a moment Chippy didn't know what to do, so she ran down to the floor, and at that point I slipped through the door and closed it behind me before she could follow.

I returned to the job of cleaning out her house, and it was

amazing how many nuts and pieces of broken shell she had been sleeping on all that time. While I worked I heard Chippy scratching at the door, and under the door I could see her little shadow racing back and forth.

When her house was completely empty and I had put all the nuts high up on a shelf in the kitchen, I opened the bedroom door and let Chippy in. She ran straight to her cage and up to her house. I saw her go into her house and hop back down onto a branch, pause and then go into her house again. She did that a couple of times, going in and coming out again, as if she thought each time she went in that she had made a mistake somehow, gone to the wrong address or something, and that if she came out and went back in again she would be right this time and this really would be her house and it wouldn't be totally empty. But finally she knew the awful truth, and she seemed to accept it. She stretched out on a branch and lay very still, and when I went over to her cage, still in my battle dress, she didn't click or growl at me. In fact she didn't even seem to notice me. It was strange to see her lying there quiet like that after such a long time of her running up and down. It was rather like looking at someone who has survived a terrible and prolonged chill and has come out of it and finally stopped shivering and chattering and lies in bed limp, exhausted and serene.

I had outsmarted Chippy. She weighed about a pound and a half; I weighed about a hundred and fifty-five. She stood about a foot high when she was up on her hind legs; I stood about five feet eight. She had a brain about the size of the end of my thumb; I had the brain that invented the H-bomb. So I had outsmarted her, but I didn't feel very smart. All I felt like was as if I had played a very dirty trick on somebody.

That was how it went for a few days. I wanted things just

to settle down squirrelwise for a little while, so I didn't let Chippy out of her cage or get involved with her much at all except to give her her regular food and clean her cage every day, and she spent most of her time sleeping in her house. When she came out of her house she would eat a few seeds or some lettuce or something and then lie for hours on a branch looking out the window. One morning I thought that enough time had passed, and I opened her cage and let her out. She went straight to the piano, disappeared behind it for a moment and came out with a walnut that looked about the size of a basketball in her mouth. She ran to her house, stuck the walnut in a corner and came out clicking and growling and in general ready to resume hostilities. I was able to close up her cage just as she sprang at the bars.

I went and got a bagful of nuts and dumped them all through the bars, covering the floor of her cage with them, knowing that this hadn't worked before and wouldn't now but really at my wit's end and wanting to do something, anything, to stop the damned clicking and growling and hysterical running up and down. More and more nuts I poured through the bars, and of course everything just got worse and worse. Finally I had to leave the house and get in my car and take a long drive, but no matter how far I got away from the house and the squirrel the problem stayed right with me. By the time I came home again I had more or less made up my mind that, once more, I was going to have to put Chippy out in the trees.

Twenty-three   THIS WAS the end of September, a little over a year since I had sent Chippy out into the world the first time, and I kept thinking of that time and putting off the inevitable. I even dressed up in my absurd costume and raided Chippy's house again, and once again she accepted what had happened and became subdued. But I couldn't stand to see her subdued. It was so terribly unlike her. It was so terribly *unsquirrelish*. And, anyway, subdued wasn't the right word for it. She was resigned, defeated and demoralized. So I completed the cycle and gave her some nuts again, and she got mean as hell again, and then I think I went through the whole thing perhaps one more time. But that was it, and one bright morning history repeated itself, and just on the spur of the moment I put down my newspaper and my cup of coffee, stood up, went over and opened the front door wide, put on my gloves, picked up Chippy in her cage and marched down the steps and across the field and put the cage down in exactly the same spot under the trees where I had put it before.

However, I resolved that from that point on everything

would be different, and it was. The time before I had made a big production out of turning Chippy loose. I had stayed out there in the field with her for hours, watching her running around in the trees until I had begun to confuse her with other squirrels and eventually had lost track of her altogether. Then, late that afternoon, when the skies had begun to darken and the wind had come up and I knew that there was going to be a storm before long, I had gone out into the field again and looked for her, wanting to see if she was all right. In the rain I had stood out there calling her name. In the darkness I had called her—not wanting her to come back, of course, nothing like that, just wanting to be sure that she could make it out there all by herself. And the next morning early I had been out there again, in the drizzle and the mosquitoes, calling and calling, and all day I had looked for her from time to time and never seen her, until evening, and then there she was all sodden on the limb of the sapodilla tree, gazing at me.

None of that this time. I opened her cage and stood back, waiting for her to come out. Of course it took a minute for her to catch on to what was happening and to realize that all she had to do was come through the door and she would be free to run up into the vast oaks that rose above her. She climbed up on top of her cage, sniffed the branch of the oak that was nearest her and then sprang onto the branch and dashed along it to the trunk of the tree. She started running around and around the trunk, sideways, showing off something awful. Then she ran all the way to the very top of the tree and paused there, looking down at me. Oh, yes, it had been fascinating to watch her running around in the oaks the last time, and she had done a lot of showing off for me then too, but now I just closed the cage and carried it away, never looking back once and feeling as if I too had just been given my freedom.

And then I shaved and took a shower and got dressed and went off in my car somewhere. I don't remember where. But I didn't come back until around noon, and that was only to have lunch. I never looked once toward the oaks on my way from the car to the house. I walked along the driveway with the light step of one who has recently had a great burden lifted from his shoulders. After lunch I went off again, and the more I had of my freedom the more I liked it. How different I was! I astounded myself. How I had changed! How I had matured! I couldn't get over it. Obviously, without even realizing it, somehow in the past year I had become quite pragmatic, quite tough, quite realistic, even hard-boiled. What a marvelous feeling to be hard-boiled! I just regretted that it hadn't happened sooner. It was an entirely different world for the hard-boiled. How wonderfully invulnerable you felt! How deliciously impervious! The hard-boiled saw everything so clearly, without the mists of sentiment to cloud their vision. For instance, I could see so clearly now how childish I had been before, hanging around in the field like a damn fool, agonizing over Chippy, worrying myself silly about her. What ghastly, quivering-lipped, sloppy, weepy, bleeding-heart sentimentality! The things it said about you! Life was so simple for the hard-boiled. We could snap our fingers at anything. Just like that! I reveled in my new self all afternoon, going visiting my friends and trying it out on them. What an *effect*.

At first, of course, knowing me, they thought it was all just a big act. "You let your squirrel go? Well, I'll be damned. But haven't we heard this song before? It seems that about this time last year . . ."

"But it's different this time," I said.

"Really?" Knowing smiles.

"Believe me," I said very quietly.

"Honest?"

"You bet."

They stared at me. "But you were so crazy about her."

"Yes, I guess I was."

"You won't be able to get along without her."

"Oh, yes, I will."

"You'll miss her terribly. You'll go and find her and bring her back."

"No," I said.

The smiles faded. They were seeing me in a fresh light, and I knew that it was a difficult moment for them. Nobody ever wants anybody else to change much. Then they think that maybe they really never knew you to start with, which is disconcerting. They feel that they will have to get to know you all over again, which might be a pain, or drop you altogether, which could be awkward.

"Look, it's no big deal," I said. "She was only a squirrel."

" 'Only a squirrel'?" they said. "Do you actually mean that?"

"Of course," I said.

Just like that!

I went home around six o'clock. Again I didn't glance even once toward the oaks as I walked along the driveway from my car to the house. I remembered that I hadn't written a word all day, so I typed a couple of words, and then I remembered that I hadn't finished the newspaper that morning, and I sat down in the living room and finished it. Then at seven o'clock the message came, so I went outside and down the steps. There was still plenty of light in the sky, but it was getting dark under the trees. A fair number of cats, half a dozen of them, were snoozing in the driveway. I walked past them, and as soon as I came around the bend by the ficus tree I saw the squirrel humping down the middle of the driveway toward me. I knew it had to be Chippy. I never saw a squirrel on the ground that late in the day. Only Chippy would have been that thoughtless. About a minute more and she would have come around the bend and found herself right in the thick of the cats, and that would have been all for her. I went toward her, and she stood up on her hind legs when we met, swaying a little as she looked up at me first with one big eye and then the other. I said this out loud: "Chippy, you know you weren't supposed to come back this time." She ignored that, and then she ran up to my shoulder, so I took her on home.

The most puzzling thing about it all was that when I had brought her cage back from the field that morning I had put it in the corner of the living room where it had always been, instead of leaving it outside somewhere. I hadn't even thought about what I was doing until I had done it, and then I had told myself that I had put it there just because I couldn't think of where else to put it at the moment. Anyway, it was there, so Chippy hopped in, and I gave her some corn, and after she had wolfed it she went straight to bed, absolutely exhausted.

Twenty-four   It's FIVE years since Chippy came back the second time. Not much has changed. I still live in the same house, and Chippy still lives here with me in her little house in her cage in the same corner of the same room. The only really big difference is that I'm married now. Chippy has accepted my wife, because Gay had the good sense to come very quickly to the same sort of understanding with her that I finally did, so we all live together in peace.

Chippy never attacks me any more. She dances for me and turns somersaults most mornings where the sunlight falls on the kitchen floor, and we have good games together, sometimes all three of us. She is, in general, quite tolerant and easygoing, which of course she can well afford to be since she certainly knows her place around here and knows that we certainly know ours and that there is no danger of any confusion on that score. Oh, there is an occasional nip and perhaps a click or a growl now and then, but it's all done with the bored air of a lioness cuffing her cubs about, not, God forbid, for anything we had actually done but just for any stray unruly or disorderly thoughts that may have crossed our minds.

The first time Chippy came back I thought it was because the storm had frightened her so much that she was even willing to give up her freedom not to have to endure another night of *that*. Then, I thought, with the passing of time, she forgot about the storm but remembered how much fun it had been to be free, and the urge to go free had come back to her and she had started attacking me again to let me know how she felt.

But when she came back the second time I didn't know what to think. There had been no storm that time. The weather had been perfect and the trees full of all kinds of fruit and acorns. So why come back to that house and that cage? Why give up the trees and the sky and the wind and all that fun out there and come humping so purposefully home along the driveway at seven?

I didn't flatter myself that she had come back to me. Of course you would like to think it's that, but I knew my squirrel too well to imagine that she was capable of overriding sentimentality. Was it corn on the cob that had brought her back then? I didn't want to think that that was it, not just her stomach, not just her taste for the kind of food that she could never find on the outside. Nor did I want to think that it was the simple security of her cage, a sort of recidivism, like ex-convicts who go and break the windows at the police station so that they can be sent back to prison, which, they have discovered, is the only place where they can feel free. But those were the two possibilities that I was left with—unless there was something else, an attraction far stronger than her belly or her cage, something totally unconscious and as irresistible as the urge to migrate or to mate. And finally it came to me, and from then on everything about Chippy's behavior in the whole time that I had known her fell into place and became logical. Chippy had come back both times because she considered my house her territory. I knew enough about squirrels by then to know that it is characteristic of them that although they may roam quite long distances during the day in search of food, at night they *must* return to their own territory and to their own nest within that territory. It is also characteristic of them that in a "territory"—an acre of woods, a corner of a city park, whatever—one squirrel is always the boss of all bosses and it is, I think, always a female. I knew all that, and yet it had never occurred to me that a squirrel could ever come to consider the inside of someone's house its territory, even though it had been raised from infancy in the house and had lived there for a long time. But I was profoundly mistaken, and so Chippy had had to attack me all those times, trying to establish once and for all her supremacy in her territory, my house, over her only rival in it, me. The nuts were just an excuse. Hard-shelled nuts are of immense value and significance to squirrels, and therefore they provided an ideal *casus belli*, but of course the real issue was always who was the boss in the house, her or me.

I believe, now, that on both her times in the woods Chippy never thought for an instant that I intended for her to *stay* out there. I think she assumed that I had just thought up the whole idea as a delightful excursion for her, a happy holiday, a little outing in the country. Super! Just the thing for a bracing day in the fall! (Why hadn't I thought of it sooner?) And, according to the scenario as she saw it, at dark I would come out there and pick her up and bring her home. The only trouble was that, the first time, she was so excited and enraptured by the experience that when I did go out there and call for her in the evening, she was either too far away by then to hear me or, like a child who is having such fun playing outdoors after supper that he can't bear to go in and chooses to ignore the voice calling him and goes on with the game, she went into one of those freezes she was so famous for. At such times I would look all over the house for her and call her, and she would just stand perfectly still and invisible on the bookcase or somewhere, gazing at me in a sappy way, as if she could *not* understand why I couldn't see her quite clearly—I'm here. What's wrong with you? Hey, you're looking right at me—instead of, for God's sake, jumping up and down to try to help me out a little. Anyway, I believe that she wanted to come home, back to her territory, but something kept us from making a connection, whether it was her fault or not. Then the storm broke and it got pitch-dark, and probably all she did for the rest of the night was cling to a limb with her tail pulled up over her, quivering, and then the next day she tried to make it home on her own. But she was still in shock from her ordeal and wasn't quite sure how to get there, and she had made it about halfway when I found her.

The second time, as I see it, was an entirely different story. She was waiting for me when it began getting on toward evening, and when I didn't show up she got impatient and just started coming along on her own, mousing right up Broadway instead of coming through the trees, off the ground, through the trees. Through the trees? That's a hassle. Cats? What cats? And who's afraid of them anyway? And I think, further, that when she saw me coming toward her along the driveway in the dusk all she really felt was mild exasperation that I hadn't come sooner.

The truth finally hit me one morning three or four days after Chippy had come back the second time. I was sitting in the living room thinking about the situation. I hadn't even let her out of her cage at all so far because I was so afraid of getting attacked again—wondering how long it was going to be this time before I had to take her out to the trees again. Suddenly it hit me, and I realized that there was no longer any question of giving Chippy her "freedom" because the only "freedom" she was interested in was the "freedom" of my house, her "territory." Thinking about it made me a little dizzy. It was a difficult adjustment to make after having thought for such a long time that in her heart Chippy had always been longing to go to her destiny in the wild.

I found myself staring at her. She was lying on a branch, in profile to me, staring back with one big eye. She would never change, I thought. There was no use hoping for that. She would never turn into a doggie or a kitty or anything else that might be a little easier to understand and to get along with, and she wouldn't even try. She would be a squirrel forever.

I got up and went into the kitchen and stood there for a minute to get away from the eye. Then I went into the bedroom and stood in there. Finally I went outside and walked around, but in the end of course I had to go back in and face it again. It was then that I acquiesced to her, in the way that one wild animal will acquiesce to another in a dispute over rights to a territory, which is really a sort of dialogue on the level of souls, and acknowledged that she was the boss in the house and that I would no longer challenge in any way her supremacy in it or ever again even think of turning her out. After that I opened her cage, and she ran all over the house, checking on everything very quickly, and then she dashed back into the living room and flung herself on me and ran all over me. But I knew that all she wanted to do was play, and I wasn't afraid that she would attack me. I never have been since then.

My wife acquiesced too when her time came. And it isn't such a bad thing actually, living in a squirrel's house. Of course we can't have much of a social life. A cocktail party or anything like that would be absolutely out of the question. Even more than one or two visitors at a time is a touchy subject. Squirrels just don't like a lot of carrying on, unless they're the ones who are doing it. No loud talking, *please,* no immoderate laughter, none of those shrieks that are so hard on one's nerves, no senseless running around, and how about let's trying to keep the stereo down to a dull roar, okay? Needless to say, smoking is frowned on, so my wife, who was once an enthusiastic smoker, finally gave it up because she got tired of having to go outside and sit on the steps every time she felt like having a coffin nail.

She had to give up some other things too. For example, her friend Spooky. Spooky was a pathetic black kitten we found abandoned one morning by the back gate. We brought him into the house and took care of him, and soon he turned into one of the handsomest animals I had ever seen, with green eyes and a gorgeous coat and big black feet. He also had the most lovable disposition I had ever seen in a cat, or any other animal for that matter.

My wife fell in love with Spooky, and of course she wanted to keep him. I wanted to keep him too, but it had been a strict rule in my house ever since Chippy had come to live with me that cats were not allowed. While Spooky seemed amazingly gentle, I was terribly aware that a cat's instincts are to catch squirrels. We kept the two of them

apart, never letting them free in the same room, but naturally there was always the danger of leaving a door ajar some day. My wife understood the situation and agreed that Spooky couldn't stay with us forever. The problem was where to find someone to give him to who would be worthy of him. We tried very hard to find someone without much luck, growing fonder of Spooky ourselves every day, and then out of a blue sky we found the ideal person.

The irony of it all was that just as I was on my way out the door to deliver Spooky to his new mistress, Chippy started bouncing around in her cage so wildly that I had to stop and look at her to see if anything was wrong. There was nothing wrong. She was simply dying to get a sniff of Spooky. They had never been close together, and she just couldn't stand it any longer. Whenever they had been in the same room I had always carried Spooky, and Chippy had almost gone out of her mind at the sight of him. I couldn't resist any longer, and I took Spooky over to her cage and held him so that one of his back paws was up against the bars. Without a moment's hesitation Chippy took hold of Spooky's paw and started trimming his nails. Squirrels are always trimming their own claws, and more often than not when I was through brushing Chippy she would pay me back by giving my fingernails a good trimming. However, I had never thought she would do it for a cat. Spooky was very patient, even though the trimming was thorough. In fact, after a while I felt him begin purring.

Anyway, it's an orderly world here, and that's something, the way things are now. Every day is more or less like every other day, things always happen more or less at the same time, and you can't really help feeling somehow that with a squirrel in charge of your territory you're very close to whoever it is who's in charge, ultimately, not only of this territory but of all the territories beyond.